CELEBRITIES' FAVOURITE FOOTBALL TEAMS

CELEBRITIES' FAVOURITE FOOTBALL TEAMS

COMPILED BY CHRIS COWLIN

FOREWORD BY SIR ALEX FERGUSON CBE

APEX PUBLISHING LTD

First published in 2007 by
Apex Publishing Ltd
PO Box 7086, Clacton on Sea, Essex, CO15 5WN, England

www.apexpublishing.co.uk

British Library Cataloguing-in-Publication Data
A catalogue record for this book
is available from the British Library

ISBN 1-904444-84-9 978-1-904444-84-8

Typeset in 10.5pt Gill Sans MT

Cover Design: Siobhan Smith

Printed and bound in Great Britain

Author's Note:
Please can you contact me - ChrisCowlin@btconnect.com - if you find any mistakes/errors in this book, as I would like to put them right on any future reprints.

Dedicated to my family;
who are always there when needed most.

FOREWORD

I am delighted to write the foreword to this book, compiled by Chris Cowlin. It is great to see how many celebrities have replied to Chris and have given their thoughts about their favourite teams and players. I was particularly pleased to see how many celebrities support Manchester United and how many past players were mentioned, most of all the late George Best.

Well, here are my memories and answers to Chris's questions:

I had quite a difficult introduction to supporting football clubs as my dad was a Celtic fan, so when my brother and I were kids my dad would take us to Celtic games. However, when we started school everything changed. As it was a Protestant school situated only 100 yards or so from Ibrox Park, everyone was a Rangers fan. So, like the rest of our school chums, we started supporting Rangers.

This was in the late 1940s and at that time Rangers had some great players – George Young, Willie Woodburn, Sammy Cox, Willie Waddell and Willie Thornton. My hero was Willie Woodburn, who was later suspended for life, sine die. I always remember one memorable game at Ibrox when they played Clyde and it turned into a real donnybrook and three players were sent off – Willie Woodburn and Billy Simpson from Rangers and Albert Murphy from Clyde. Rumour had it at the time that there was a feud between Simpson of Rangers, who was from Belfast, and Murphy of Clyde, who was from Dublin, such was the religious feeling in the west of Scotland at that time.

I always remember after that game I was waiting outside the stadium trying to get autographs from my heroes and approached Sammy Cox, who was talking to his brother I think, and he was swearing like a trooper, calling the referee for everything. I was absolutely shocked and when I got home told my father I had heard Sammy Cox swearing. You see, even then we didn't expect our heroes to be anything but gods, and it hasn't changed today.

When I got to about nine or ten, I started to diversify in terms of watching football, and when Rangers were away from home I would go to watch my local junior team, which at the time was equivalent to the conference league in England. They were called Benburb FC, affectionately known as 'the Bens' or 'the Chooky Hens' in Govan Doric language. I absolutely loved them and to this day I get their match programme sent to me every week. It was great fun listening to the old pensioners stationed around the railings at the front of the terracing, venting their spleens about the players and referees and particularly the poor linesmen. I don't know how many times a walking stick hit the backside of one of the linesmen if he gave a bad decision or tried to trip him up as he was running up the line. Those old guys loved their football team!

My heroes of that team were Nicholson, the centre half, and the two wingers, Dunky Rae and Tommy Douglas. As the years wore on and I reached 16, I used to train with the Bens along with some other promising boys from the local school, Govan High Secondary. There were six of us and every one of them became senior players. There were the McKinnon twins, Ronnie and Donnie: Ronnie signed for Rangers at 17 and played for about 12 years as their regular centre half, and also for Scotland; and his brother, Donnie, played for Partick Thistle and then became a physiotherapist with the Scotland under-21 eleven. My own brother, Martin, went on to play for Partick Thistle, Morton, Barnsley and Doncaster Rovers. The other two were Jim Morrison, who played for Clyde, and Craig Watson, who played for Rangers for a spell and then Morton and Falkirk.

The irony of this story is that there was a change in the team committee of Benburb FC and new people came in to turn round the fortunes of the club. We were all called into an office at the ground to be told by the manager that we had no future at Benburb FC and would no longer be allowed to train with them. He was going to rely on experience - well he knew his football!

I'll always remember that moment as we all came out of the ground together and stood outside, feeling a bit lost, and one of us said, "What are we going to do?" Ronnie McKinnon then flippantly joked, "I'm ready to play for Rangers". Well, it didn't turn out to be a joke, as Ronnie then signed for a junior team from outside Glasgow called Dunipace. He was only there for four months before being signed by Rangers, which just goes to show how thin the dividing line is between success and failure.

These memories will always stay with me. And to think that I later went on to play for my boyhood heroes, Rangers, their ground so close to home that from the main stand you could look into my mother's window!

I suppose the real message is that you should never lose hope or give in. Perseverence and holding on to what you believe in and want to be will help you get there.

It is wonderful that Chris Cowlin has decided to donate all his royalties for this book to a great cause - The Willow Foundation, which was founded by Bob and Megs Wilson in memory of their daughter, Anna, who died of cancer aged 31. It is a registered charity dedicated to improving the quality of life of seriously ill young adults aged 16 to 40 throughout the UK, by organising and funding a 'Special Day' of their choice.

I hope you like looking through the book - enjoy!

Sir Alex Ferguson CBE

ACKNOWLEDGEMENTS

Vicki Adamson, Avril Bank (The Willow Foundation), Frances Banks, Les Batin, Jackie Bright (Apex Publishing Ltd), Tel Currie, Marc De La Roche, Clair Emmerson (Ipswich Town Football Club), June Ford-Crush, Julia Forsyth, Samantha Funning, Mike Hallowell, Tim Helm, Peter Martin (www.ffsp.railwayinn.me.uk), Adrian Milne, Colin Mitchell (Shoot Magazine), Anna Moorby, Karen Nicholls (Talk Forty Four), Rachel Phillips, Alison Prince, Nicola Regan, Jo Royce (Gordon and French), Pooja Shah, Hilary Smith (Manchester United Football Club), Dave Tennant, Kathryn Walsh, Chris Williams (Oxford United Football Club), David Williams (The Willow Foundation), Linda Yaffe, Jon Willis (Football Careers Centre).

INTRODUCTION

I sent out over 500 letters and e-mails asking celebrities these questions:

1. What is your favourite football team and why?
2. Who were/are your favourite players past/present?

I had always wondered which celebrities supported what clubs, and have to admit that the replies from some of them were a complete surprise. For others, I already knew who they supported, but my enquiries brought forth plenty of additional interesting information.

I also decided to donate ALL of my author royalties to The Willow Foundation charity, which was set up by Bob Wilson and his wife Megs in 1999. It is one of my favourite charities, so for me there was no hesitation in making this decision.

I would personally like to thank Sir Alex Ferguson CBE for writing the foreword to this book and taking time out from his busy schedule to help on this project.

While compiling this book I spoke to and met various celebrities, which was a fantastic experience - a particular highlight being a 40-minute phone conversation with Jim Bowen. I thoroughly enjoyed our chat, Jim, so thanks very much indeed for your time!

Thanks also must go to EVERY person who took the time to reply to me. There are many A, B and C list celebrities in this book, together with the odd Z list celeb ... but, whoever you are, your contribution is very much appreciated. I would also like to say a BIG thank you to Tel Currie. I must say that some of the celebrities I approached and of whom I am a great fan sadly did not respond, which was very disappointing.

I do hope you enjoy this book - compiling it was a real pleasure!

In closing, I would like to thank all my friends and family for their encouragement in bringing this project to fruition.

Best wishes
Chris Cowlin

PETER ALLISS

GOLF COMMENTATOR

I have very catholic tastes in my affection for various football clubs, far too many to mention. The reason for that is I spent my formative years in the Bournemouth area and the nearest first-class football was at Portsmouth. Bournemouth and Boscombe were in the Third Division South, and Southampton flitted between that division and the Second, with no big-name players in view. BUT I did for a period train at the Boscombe football ground when Bill McGarry was the manager. He had played for England as a wing half in a 'B' international, was a great enthusiast and had success whilst at the club; similarly with Harry Redknapp in later years.

Bournemouth is a delightful ground with a superb playing surface, and the club flattered to deceive on a number of occasions. They were always entertaining and welcoming.

In 1980 I moved to Leeds where I was introduced to their football team and also rugby league; both clubs were at the top of their form at that period, Leeds United, in fact, fielding 11 internationals most Saturdays.

Now I live on the Surrey/Hampshire border and am attracted to the Aldershot Football Club, which I am told has the largest playing surface of any club, certainly in England and maybe in the British Isles - strange but, I'm told, true. Each year they try for promotion to get back into league football, from which they dropped many years ago when they went into receivership, and hopefully they will make it back one day.

Good luck with the book.

MAURICE AMDUR

INTERNATIONAL CELEBRITY CLAIRVOYANT

My team was Arsenal. My favourite player was George Best.

I now feel football is all money politics and big business. I don't really care for football anymore, but I also remember Pelé with fondness and respect as today's players are mostly like soap actors: instantly forgettable and fake.

I would like to wish you good luck and God bless.

BOB ANDERSON

PROFESSIONAL DARTS PLAYER

My favourite team is Middlesbrough, because of all the friends I have made in the Teeside area.

My favourite recent player is Mark Schwartzer.

My boyhood heroes were Jimmy Greaves and Geoff Hurst.

JEFFREY ARCHER
AUTHOR & PLAYWRIGHT

My favourite team, I would have to say, is England, and my favourite players were Jimmy Greaves, Bobby Moore and Nobby Stiles.

Best of luck with the charity book.

OSSIE ARDILES
FORMER FOOTBALLER

My favourite team is the Argentinean side Boca Juniors.

SARAH ASH

AUTHOR

The football team we support is Crystal Palace Football Club (our recently retired headmaster is a great and lifelong supporter!), so that's where my allegiances would lie.

PADDY ASHDOWN

MP

My favourite team is Yeovil Town - of course - being an ex-MP for Yeovil! I wouldn't like to choose one of their players as it would be divisive. Thank you for asking. Good luck with the book.

ROBIN ASKWITH

ACTOR

My favourite team is Queens Park Rangers.

Why? They trained near my school - Merchant Taylors' - where football (soccer) was banned! Any boy seen playing with round balls in the quad will be beaten!

My favourite player was Stan Bowles. For a while we went out with sisters and knew each other well.

MICHAEL ASPEL

PRESENTER

I'm afraid I'm not a dedicated football fan, although Stanley Matthews was a boyhood hero, because he was a clean player and a decent man. I'm a great admirer of Thierry Henry because of his delicacy and finesse.

My favourite team would have to be Fulham, because my youngest son is a fan.

Good luck with the book.

RICHARD BACON

MP

As a schoolboy I supported Norwich City, which my grandfather used to take me to watch, and also Chelsea. Now Norwich is my local team so they still get my vote. Nowadays I'm not a huge football fan but I can still scream at the television with the best of them when the World Cup is on!

As for an individual player, I still think George Best was the most sublime I have ever seen. It was just beautiful to watch. He was touched by genius - and the attending demons!

GEOFF BARKER

AUTHOR

My favourite football team (US) was the Chicago Bears. I watched with youthful enthusiasm years ago when they and their dynamic coach Mike Ditka mowed down the team on the way to the Superbowl. Of course every young guy's favourite player was the superhuman quarterback Walter Paten, whose astoundingly athletic performance saw me drag my skinny butt down the gym day in, day out, for years.

When it comes to Aussie teams, who can beat the passion of the Socceroos? Australians play everything with a passion that makes it that much harder to become a stand-out player. So I'll just say I love them all, but oh so much more when they win!

NICK BATEMAN

TV PRESENTER

My favourite team is Fulham and it has been for many years, although in the late eighties/early nineties I went to Chelsea and Fulham home games as they played on alternate Saturdays. When the shed at Stamford Bridge was taken down, I followed Fulham exclusively around the United Kingdom and was on the team coach for the Carlisle and Mansfield games which saw Mickey Adams and Fulham win promotion to the Second Division. Rod Mcree's goal at Carlisle and Mickey Conroy's goal from the halfway line against Wycombe Wanderers are the best goals I have seen at Fulham, as well as Paul Moody against Preston NE.

My footballing heroes when I was very young were Alan Hansen, Kenny Daglish, Terry McDermott and Jimmy Case. I supported Liverpool for a couple of years. My favourite all-time player was Bob Wardle, the Shrewsbury goalkeeper, as I wrote to him when I was ten and he replied in depth; you just would not get that now.

I still look out for Fulham, although I gave up my season ticket there six years ago. I miss the club as it was, struggling and grateful for funds. These days I spend more time watching Lincoln City or Shrewsbury Town, as this to me is real football, watched by real fans.

Best ground for food: Cambridge United (bacon sandwich). Awful grounds: Oldham, Doncaster and Wigan's old ground, Springfield Park.

JEREMY BATES

FORMER TENNIS PLAYER

My favourite team - there's only one - Stoke City FC. Aunts and uncles all lived up there and some still do. When I was 8 I was taken to my first game at the old Victoria ground. I can't really remember who they played, but I've stuck with them ever since. I've been to a couple of games this season and was very kindly taken onto the pitch before the Watford game in Sept '05 with the sponsors for pre-match photos - memory of a lifetime to be out there with a huge crowd - kindly organised by Tony Pullis after his wife came over to Wimbledon. Britannia Stadium is awesome and I drive up for home games sometimes, as the website is great to get tickets for where you want to sit.

Tough to choose a favourite player: Hudson, Greenhoff, Shilton, etc., when i started going; and the current ones - Lawrence is playing well, Hendrie too, but they are new, and I don't see them often enough to make a judgement really, Hoefkens I like and Russell, as they really get stuck in.

JEREMY BEADLE

TV PRESENTER

My favourite football team is Arsenal, which is out of loyalty to the Directors. My favourite player was Ian Wright.

My boyhood heroes were Sherlock Holmes, Nat Lofthouse and Allan Quartermain.

Good luck with the book.

JACK BENNETT
ACTOR

Having been born in Nottingham, having parents from Lancashire and Wales, and spending most of my childhood growing up in the West Midlands there was only ever going to be one team for me -Liverpool.

If truth be told, my dad did his best to convince me that his beloved Manchester City were the team that I should give my heart to, adding one more voice to the chorus of 'Blue Moon' on the Kippax. His cunning plan was foiled when he took my sister and me (both still at a very innocent age) to see the Sky Blues play Notts County. The game wasn't much to write home about, but we both remember seeing a guy a few rows in front of us have a couple of his fingers removed by some thug. Not such a beautiful game. I've always been a bit of a bad luck charm for City, whenever my dad's reluctantly allowed me to join him, but do have a favourite memory of seeing the stalwart City keeper Eric Nixon lose his rag in a game against Crystal Palace and flatten the Eagles bovver boys Mark Bright and Ian Wright.

But back to the team at the other end of the Lancashire Road. There was one reason why they were to be the club my happiness was to be pinned to for the rest of my life. It wasn't the decades of unrivalled success. Nor the multiple successes in Europe. Not the fact that the two most outstanding managers in history had been at the helm of this magnificent club (and to the United fans out there, I'll grudgingly admit that Ferguson has done a decent job but he's no Shankly or Paisley). No, my love was secured by one man - John Barnes.

Barnsey was, and remains, the most beautiful thing I have ever seen on a football pitch. Hurdling vicious sliding tackles on the left wing, cutting in from the right flank onto that deadly left peg, dropping the ball perfectly onto Aldridge's head, exchanging one-twos with the little magician Peter Beardsley ... Poetry in motion. Of course it never really happened for him with England, save a few moments of ingenuity (that goal in Brazil, single-handedly taking the fight to the Argies when he came on in '86, a brute of a volley against Chile). But that didn't matter to me.Those idiots in the crowd at Wembley who used to jeer his every touch didn't know what I did. They couldn't see that here was our Maradona, our Jairzinho. But that's another story.

There have been other heroes for me. Robbie Fowler and Jamie Redknapp in the mid-'90s, and more recently it's Jamie Carragher and Stevie Gerrard. But Barnsey's the one who started it all. What a player, what a team, what a history. Sorry dad.

DICKIE BIRD

FORMER CRICKET UMPIRE

Here are a few thoughts about my favourite football team: I am a season ticket holder at Barnsley Football Club. I have been a season ticket holder for many years and I have supported them for 68 years, which is a long time.

When I left school I signed for Barnsley Football Club and in the summer I played for Barnsley Cricket Club. I decided to stick with cricket and I am glad I did. The rest is history - I played county cricket for Yorkshire CCC and also Leicestershire CCC before going into umpiring.

While at school I played with Tommy Taylor, the best centre forward I have ever seen, and I have seen all the great centre forwards from Lawton right through to Owen. He was the finest header of a football I have ever seen, he was two footed, right on left foot, and he also had great pace. He used to hang in the air when he headed the ball. He sadly lost his life in the Manchester United air disaster.

Tommy played for Barnsley before he went to United and of course he was my favourite player at Oakwell. When we were boys we used to practise together for hours on end on very rough ground scattered with broken glass - it made us hungry for success and to go on and make a living in sport.

Tommy's father and my father both worked at the same coalface in Barnsley. He was a close friend at school and he was so sadly missed - I lost a true friend.

So, Barnsley Football Club is my favourite team, and wherever I have been in the world I've always looked for the Barnsley result; it has always been that way.

I have seen some great players at Oakwell. The best all-round footballer I have ever seen without a shadow of a doubt is Tom Finney of Preston North End and England. I put him alongside the likes of Diego Maradona, Pelé and George Best. He had everything a footballer should have; like all greats he had a gift and that is balance.

One of my other favourite players at Barnsley was Johnny Kelly who played outside left. He was very good with his left and right foot, and used to go inside and outside with pace. He was marvellous to watch. I once saw him give Alf Ramsey the biggest run around he'd ever had - Barnsley beat Tottenham Hotspur 5-1, or it may have been Southampton.

Some other great players I have seen at Oakwell are Wilf Mannion of Middlesbrough, the best inside forward I have ever seen, and Neil Franklin of Stoke City, the best centre half ever.

I have some wonderful memories of Barnsley and the fine players I saw play at Oakwell, memories that I shall always treasure.

Chris, I wish you every success with the book; it is for a tremendous cause.

JASMINE BIRTLES

FINANCIAL EXPERT & TV PRESENTER

I'm a fan of the Seagulls - Brighton and Hove Albion. I have to be. I grew up near Brighton, went to the Brighton and Hove High School and really the only team one was supposed to support (in an all-girls school) at the time was the Seagulls. My dad took me to a couple of games as a child and I remember taking a book with me in case I got bored. I didn't get bored but I was a bit cold and wondered why we had to stand for the whole thing. The star striker at the time was Peter Ward - a good-looking guy with a regulation '70s footballer-style tight perm. His name particularly sticks in my mind because the fans used to sing a ditty about him every time he did something impressive. I thought it went: 'He's short, he's bald, it must be Peter Ward ... Peter Waaaard'. In fact it was: 'He's shot, he's scored, it must be Peter Ward ... Peter Waaaard'! I like my version best.

ROGER BLACK

FORMER OLYMPIC ATHLETE

My favourite football team is Southampton because a friend of my father took me to see them in 1976, my first professional game. It has subsequently caused many jokes at my expense as I was born and bred in Portsmouth.

My favourite players were Mick Shannon, Kevin Keegan and Peter Osgood.

JIM BOWEN
TV PRESENTER

My favourite football team is Blackburn Rovers. I was brought up with them and I went to watch them before Jack Walker was there and made his millions before the stadium we have now.

I used to go there when it cost half a crown and when a tackle below the neck was legal! Half a crown - twelve-and-a-half new pence! I used to watch from the enclosure at the ground. Jack Walker stood on the terraces next to us fans - he was a scrap metal man and loved the club; he put a lot of money in the club unlike chairmen like Swailes and Chelsea's Bates.

The first match I went to watch was Blackburn Rovers against Wolves. The pitches were not like the bowling greens now.

I used to support Burnley, whom Blackburn supporters refer to as 'The Dingles' - a race riot; a tribal race not racist. I started watching Burnley when I lived in Elton. I used to go with my dad and stand on the halfway line, near the tunnel. I remember once player Reg Hatwell was running out with his ankle boots on and steel toecaps, in a First Division match - smoking a fag! He put the cigerette out about a yard from the pitch with smoke pouring out of his mouth - that's how fit they were then. Some of the players were in the pub until 1 a.m. The kick-offs were at 3 p.m. and some players were in the pub before the matches - can you imagine that now?

I taught PE for ten years and did a bit of the coaching badge. I was never a great player but did understand the game quite well and kept up with it. But the game and tactics have really moved on nowadays. I appreciate the incredible talent now. Any team of my era would be 20 goals down by half-time against any of today's teams: the speed, skill, fitness level, playing surface are so much better, and the lighter ball - you can do so much more with it. I go to watch Blackburn when I can. It is always the first result I look for.

I became president at Morecambe - not because I supported them but because I was famous. It all started when Morecambe beat Cambridge and got Ipswich Town in the FA Cup. I knew a lot of the board and the press found out, so they thought it was a good idea - because I was well known the press would turn up and give them a bit of national coverage. It was lovely for the club. However, when the Morecambe fans found out I supported Blackburn Rovers they e-mailed the club and asked why I was president, so I said I could do without the grief and resigned from the post. I was president for around three years, but the Morecambe fans did not want a Blackburn Rovers supporter as president. I still have a lot of time for the club and the board though, and still go to the dinners and have drinks with them all. What a story - a failed president! It was nice to see how passionate some of the youngsters were at the club - very dedicated.

Football nowadays in all about money. However, I think David Beckham's move to the USA is excellent; he has always acted very well. There are a lot of fallen players - George Best, Paul Gascoigne - we can go on, can't we? Let's hope Wayne Rooney don't go the same way.

The Premier League is now at an awesome level with some fantastic matches - the speed of the game is so fast. The live games are a phenomenal advert for the Premier League.

As my favourite player of all time, I would have to say Bestie - George Best. He was so sadly wasted as he had so much talent. My favourite player of recent times is Cristiano Ronaldo. He's unbelievable as a soccer player - disgracefully skilful! Hopefully in the future he will grow into a gentleman. An awesome player! I suppose there are always some cracks in the make-up when you're as talented as he is. I am an Englishman and therefore support England in the national championships and World Cups. I wear a badge with pride on all my nice suits! I think in a few years' time we will not be allowed to display the England flags, etc., like people currently do outside their houses and on their cars. At my age I can say that mine is an old man's protest - I will wear my badge!

It is great to see that Sir Alex Ferguson has written the foreword to the book and a charity is benefiting from the sales.

JOHN BOYNE

AUTHOR

My favourite moment in football was during the Italia '90 World Cup on 25 June, when my national side, Ireland, was playing Romania in the second round for a place in the quarter-finals. Ireland had never qualified for the World Cup before and Jack Charlton's enthusiasm and take-no-prisoners attitude had swept the entire country up into a state of excitement.

The three matches in the first round were incredibly exciting. First, we drew 1-1 with our old adversaries England, when Kevin Sheedy scored a late equaliser in the 73rd minute to tie the match. Six days later, a disappointing 0-0 draw with Egypt left us with everything to play for in the third match. Holland came into the match with the same results as Ireland, a 1-1 draw and a 0-0 draw, and went 1-0 up in the tenth minute. However, Niall Quinn levelled the match in the 71st minute, which left both Ireland and Holland with equal points and goal differences. The second-place spot was drawn by lots and we were lucky enough to get through.

The second round match was against Romania and ended in another 0-0 draw, which left the whole country on tenterhooks as the penalty shoot-out began. Sheedy, the hero of the England game scored first, then Hegi scored for Romania: 1-1. Houghton and Lupu scored: 2-2. Townsend and Rotariu made it 3-3. More goals from Cascarino and Lupescu for 4-4. How long would this go on? How much could the country take?!

David O'Leary stepped up to take the fifth penalty for Ireland and scored. A miss from the Romanians and it would all be over. Timofte walked towards the penalty spot and drove the ball into the welcoming hands of Packie Bonner and the match was over.

Ireland was through to the quarter-finals of the World Cup - where we got beat 1-0 by Italy. But still - it remains the most exciting day in Irish footballing history and no manager since then has equalled what Jack Charlton achieved.

DOUG BRADLEY

ACTOR

Favourite team: Liverpool. A born and bred scouser, my heart has beaten for the mighty Red Men all my life.

LIAM BRADY

FORMER FOOTBALLER

My favourite team is Arsenal.

KENNETH BRANAGH

ACTOR

My favourite team is Tottenham Hotspur and has been for as long as I remember - 5 or 6 years old.

Why? Danny Blanchflower, Dave Mackay and the double-winning team of 1960/1961.

Like all Tottenham fans I live in hope of repeating the double before I drop off the twig.

Good luck with the book and your fund-raising for The Willow Foundation.

JO BRAND

COMEDIENNE & TV PRESENTER

Your questions are not difficult to answer, but I have to say that I do not spend Saturday afternoons glued to the scorecards as they come in. Actually I still have childhood horrors of the then interminable amount of time it took whilst the teams and scores were droned out - waiting for Dr Who! Remember - and it was in black and white!

Being a Southerner (South of England dweller) you had to look to the London clubs for a team and my long-term allegiance has been as follows:

My favourite team - no question - and I am an official supporter, if my subs are paid up: Crystal Palace Football Club.

My favourite player - still no question about it: Ian Wright.

It would be indiscreet of me to reveal too much about my girlhood heroes, if you don't mind, but who could resist the charms of Ilya Kuryakin in the opening sequence of 'The Man From U.N.C.L.E.', but then he wasn't best known for his slide tackles was he?

MARK BRIGHT

FORMER FOOTBALLER

My favourite football team is Port Vale.

CHARLES BRONSON

INFAMOUS PRISIONER

My favourite football team is Luton Town - Come on you Hatters!

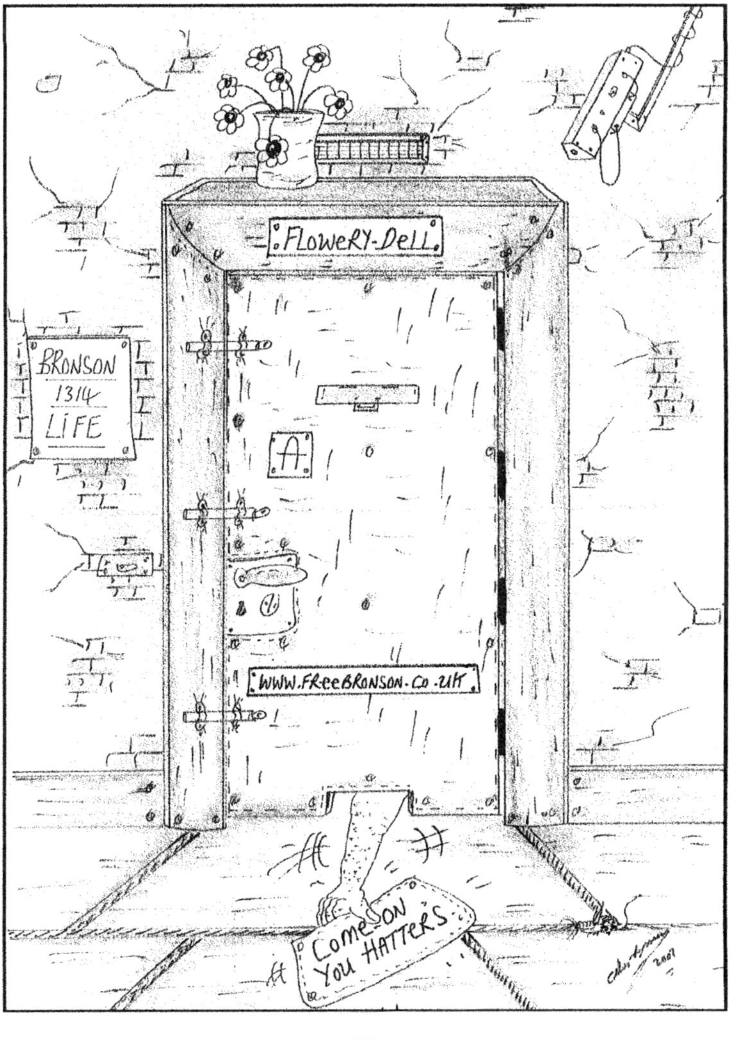

ADGER BROWN

COMPERE & COMEDIAN

My favourite football team is Portsmouth.

GEORGE BURLEY

FOOTBALL MANAGER

It is difficult to pick out a favourite team, but needless to say the results that matter most to me are those of Southampton Football Club.

As regards favourite players, I would have to say John Gregg of Rangers and Pelé.

JOHN BURTON

ACTOR

It is strange as I have done a number of magazine interviews over the years along with TV and radio interviews (probably hundreds rather than thousands) and only ONCE have I been asked this question - so here goes!

I am an absolutely avid and mad Ipswich Town fan and have been since 1974 (four years before we won the FA Cup). The glory years were the '80s when we won pretty much everything and the only uncapped international player in the team was goalkeeper Paul Cooper.

My favourite players were Alan Brazil (whom I listen to most days on Talksport radio) and Paul Mariner, but the team was awesome, and to say that a 'small' club like mine can boast two England managers in Sir Alf Ramsay and Sir Bobby Robson ain't half bad.

The team of the day was: Paul Cooper, George Burley, Mick Mills (capt), Frans Thijssen, Russell Osman, Terry Butcher, John Wark, Arnold Muhren, Paul Mariner, Alan Brazil and Eric Gates.

All the best and good luck with all your work.

DAVID CAMERON

MP

I support Aston Villa – it was the team I watched first. I have to admit that I am a bit of a fair-weather friend and not a devotee.

My favourite player? Andy Gray is the one I remember from the past and I enjoy his punditry. Recently, I like watching a range of people - Frank Lampard, Ryan Giggs and, along with half of the country, Wayne Rooney.

MENZIES CAMPBELL

MP

My favourite team has to be Scotland, whose fortunes I have followed since I was quite young. To be a Scotland supporter requires a philosophical outlook on life! You also need a keen sense of history to remember those occasional periods when the team has performed well!

Scotland supporters travel hopefully, are sometimes disappointed but remain unquenchably optimistic. It's a bit like politics I suppose.

My hero was the late great Jim Baxter who in his prime was probably one of the best players in the world.

KAREN CARNEY

LADIES ENGLAND INTERNATIONAL FOOTBALLER

As if my team is Birmingham City because I'm from Birmingham and all my family are blue-nose fans!

My favourite players are Cristiano Ronaldo because he's so exciting and there is more to come from him, and Steven Gerrard because of how passionate he is for his club - Liverpool!

JOHN CHALLIS
ACTOR

As it happens, Bob Wilson is one of my all-time favourite players - for, as you can guess, my favourite team is Arsenal and always has been since I was about five years old. I have no connection with North London whatsoever. I was in fact born in Bristol and always look out for the Rovers and City results!

Another great goalkeeper the Gunners had was Jack Kelsey - yes, I do go back that far! This was the team, I think, I was really first aware of for Arsenal - Logie, Lishman, Roper - I think Kelsey was the keeper for that team? Latterly George Eastham has been a favourite, David Herd another - that first double side - Radford, Kennedy, Charlie George, Frank McLintock with Bob Wilson in goal! Later, Sunderland, Stapleton, Brady, Rix.

Most recently of course the Wenger sides, inheriting that great defence - Winterburn, Dixon, Bould and Adams - and Alan Smith, the most elegant header of a ball I ever saw. Then Limpar, Overmars, Bergkamp, and now Henry, Fabregas and Little Walcott should become a hero!

Also, I remember Highbury itself with great fondness; it was just different - the art deco design, the clock, the police band. I was sorry to see it go. Football has changed, the world has changed, but the memories remain, thank God! I was lucky enough to go 'backstage' on a couple of occasions: once to meet George Graham - another special player in that first double side and of course a redoubtable manager; on the second to meet David Seaman, yet another goalkeeper, and a true gentleman!

ADRIAN CHILES

SPORTS TV PRESENTER

My team's West Brom. I loved my grandad and he loved the Albion so I loved the Albion too. I first went in April 1974. Tony Brown was my favourite player at first, but he was soon supplanted by Cyrille Regis. But basically I still love the Albion more and more every day. I just can't help it.

I also support Croatia, because that's where my mum's from.

MARTIN CHIVERS

FORMER FOOTBALLER

My favourite football team is Real Madrid.

TOM CLARKE-HILL

ACTOR

My favourite football team is the Oakland Raiders.

At the age of 14 when I was living in Northern California, the 1968 Oakland Raiders had two great quarterbacks, Daryle Lamonica and veteran George Blanda. George only played once in a while as quarterback but when he did his completion average was way higher than Daryles - George also was the extra point and field goal kicker. I was pretty loyal to the Raiders but also admired the boys across the bay - the San Francisco 49ers, who in '68 had a killer QB named John Brodie.

Fast forward to 1986 - the Oakland Raiders were now the LA Raiders and I was the bass player in the big band at the Oakland Coliseum. My favourite player then was the great running back Marcus Allen, but the band spent more time watching the Raiderettes (cheerleaders) - 52 top-heavy babes who were NOT hired for their dancing ability! I just watched the music on my stand and the game though - honest!

PAUL COIA

TV PRESENTER & BROADCASTER

As I grew up my favourite team was Celtic, probably because that's who everyone else at school supported. My dad never took me to a game as he thought football was a waste of a good Saturday afternoon, so all my heroes were admired from afar.

My special hero was Bobby Lennox, one of the Lisbon Lions which became the first British team to win the European Cup, under Jock Stein. He was so fast and could dribble brilliantly, and he was the first I can remember to introduce the 'step over' in Scottish football (or perhaps he just had wobbly legs!) Even though his teammate Jimmy Johnstone was more showy and difficult to predict, Lennox was the better all-round footballer for me.

I met most of the Lisbon Lions at some stage or other later in life and I spent one charity evening with a few who were still talking over their memories all those years on, almost as if time had stood still for them.

I've been lucky to meet many Celtic heroes, from Billy McNeil and Tommy Gemmell through to Kenny Dalglish and Danny McGrain, but never, ever, Bobby Lennox. There's still time isn't there?

Good luck raising loads of money for the charity.

NORMAN COOK (FATBOY SLIM)

DJ & MUSIC PRODUCER

Good luck with the project. Here is my contribution:

After a childish fascination with Leeds United in the Bremner/Lorimer era (never went, but they always won and everyone at my school supported Chelsea), in the early 1980s I moved to Brighton and have supported Brighton & Hove Albion ever since. I am currently sponsor and director (for my troubles). I support them because whether we are good or not they are ours and I go to every home game when I'm in the country. Also we are never dull - the term 'mid-table' doesn't exist in our vocabulary. We recently spent five seasons in different leagues - promotion, relegation, play-offs, even one champions' cup, it's always a rollercoaster!

My favourite player: Johnny Crumplin. Not the best player I've seen, but so entertaining to watch. His headers back to our keeper had more power than our strikers at the other end. He also fell over a lot, which I always enjoy!

SIR HENRY COOPER, OBE KSG

FORMER EUROPEAN, BRITISH & COMMONWEALTH HEAVYWEIGHT BOXING CHAMPION

My favourite team was and is Arsenal. I fought for my World Title at their ground many years ago and have been a keen follower of the Arsenal team ever since!

I wish you every success with your book to raise monies for The Willow Foundation.

JUDY CORNWELL

ACTRESS

In the early nineteen-fifties my uncle, Ronald McCullen, used to play for Battersea. Later on, when he moved to Seaford, Sussex, he used to play there. Living in Brighton, I used to go along to the old Albion football ground and yell "Seagulls" with every other Brightonian. But having being brought up for a good part of my formative years in Australia, whenever the world football matches are being played I cheer for Australia or England. If they play each other I sit silently and whisper, "May the best team win".

Among the English teams, my favourite has always been Manchester United. But I am hoping Brighton will eventually get its own stadium and I can once again yell "Seagulls".

Good luck with your book.

TONY COTTEE

FORMER FOOTBALL PLAYER

I had two favourite teams as a boy. The first was the West Ham team that beat Fulham 2-0 in the 1975 FA Cup final (I was 10 years old and didn't go to the game), and the second was the team that beat Arsenal 1-0 in the 1980 FA Cup final, a game I did attend as a 15-year-old supporter. I'm sure you'll be able to choose one of the teams and get the line-ups, but if you want to pin me down - the 1980 team and Brooking and Devonshire would be my favourites.

My hero as a kid was Bryan 'Pop' Robson who played in two spells at West Ham United and for Newcastle United and Sunderland. I used to watch him closely playing alongside David Cross and tried to model my game on him as we were of a similar height and build. I have had the pleasure of meeting him on several occasions in the last few years and he is a nice bloke as well!

Wayne Rooney is my favourite at the moment.

DAVE COURTNEY OBE

CELEBRITY GANGSTER & AUTHOR

I live just five minutes away from the original Woolwich Arsenal, the birthplace of the Arsenal Football Club, which is in London of course. I have supported the Gunners all my life, as did my father. Best moment: beating Liverpool to win The Championship.

Best players: Liam Brady and Thierry Henry.

The team ooze class and you can't buy class, and I also have to admit to having had one of my most memorable sexual experiences whilst in one of the boxes at a Tottenham v. Arsenal match, in which Arsenal won and I pleased the crowds.

CHRIS COWLIN

AUTHOR OF VARIOUS FOOTBALL BOOKS & COMPILER OF THIS BOOK

My favourite team as a small child was Liverpool. I supported them because they were one the best teams around at that time. My favourite player from the side was Ian Rush as he scored all the goals.

I then started to support Spurs ('Glory, Glory, Tottenham Hotspur'), not because they were the best team but because of their tradition and the way they played.

My dad Martin and I always went to see Spurs play, but not so much now because of work commitments, etc. We would both agree that the best player that ever graced White Hart Lane for us was Jurgen Klinsmann - a true genius and a workhorse. So many stories came with him when Alan Sugar brought him to England in 1994, but he proved everyone wrong! It would be great to see Jurgen as manager of Spurs one day, as his commitment to football and Spurs was second to none.

I was very fortunate to meet Jurgen, and he was a true gent, as have been many of the players that I have met over the past few years.

I have witnessed some fantastic matches at 'The Lane' and saw some great players and many managers come and go. Another great memory is of the time that Spurs beat Nottingham Forest in the FA Cup final in 1991 and Arsenal in the semi-final with goals from Gazza and Lineker.

The most disappointed I have ever been was a few years ago when my friend Paul and I travelled to Wales to see the League Cup final at the Millennium Stadium and Spurs lost 2-1 to Blackburn Rovers - it is probably the best game I have ever watched live, as the atmosphere was electric! Brad Friedal had a great game in goal for them.

Spurs have always had great players, some favourites of mine being: Danny Blanchflower, Gary Mabbutt, David Ginola and Teddy Sheringham.

Nowadays, I am more of a 'general' fan of football. I go to a lot of matches and travel all over the country. I also enjoy writing about football, delving into the history of clubs, seeing what interesting facts I can dig up. You will notice at the back of this book that I have written quiz books on

West Ham, Arsenal, Colchester United, Norwich City and Watford. These have received fantastic backing from past and present players and sales on all the books raise money for charity.

IAN CULLEN

ACTOR

My team is and always has been Sunderland - my home town. I always admired Len Shackleton - firstly because he was very gentle with young fans and secondly because I just loved his unforgettable name.

EDWINA CURRIE

MP

I am not really a footie fan. I watched the World Cup a bit but was quite relieved (and not surprised) when England fell out - some of those other teams had real talent whereas we seemed to have talked ourselves up too much and our talented players (e.g., Rooney) need to get their tempers under control. It was nice when normal life returned!

TEL CURRIE

BOXING PROMOTER & AUTHOR

My favourite team are QPR. I am a West Londoner who has lived very close to the Bush. I started going to Loftus Road when Terry Venables was manager and we had a plastic pitch. There was also one of the most delicious pie, mash 'n' eel shops on the Goldhawk Road.

I would also watch Brentford at Griffin Park. At this time, Brentford had one of my QPR heroes and genius Stan Bowles as well as Ron 'Chopper' Harris. Tony Currie is also a distant relative, so QPR were a family team really.

My favourite players are the entertainers, real characters that you just don't get anymore. Men like Stan Bowles, Rodney Marsh and Tony Currie were pure genius. The best player ever, though, had to be George Best - he was a typical genius, a man who was untouchable at what he did, but his life was plagued by unhappiness and of course chronic alcoholism. Real geniuses are never happy people; it always comes with a price. Can you imagine what Besty would be worth today with the money players are on?

The seventies was the time when great players only got a few caps for England because the likes of Bowles, Marsh, Currie, Osgood and Worthington were virtuosos who wouldn't melt into a negative system.

I have heard the word genius used in terms of average players like Beckham. Anyone who thinks Beckham is genius should take a look at videos of the players I have mentioned. Beckham isn't fit to lick George Best's boots clean!

STEVE DAVIS
FORMER SNOOKER WORLD CHAMPION

My favourite team is the London side Leyton Orient.

JIM DAWKINS
AUTHOR

Much of my early childhood was spent travelling the country as my father was in the RAF, so I didn't have a base where I could support a local team. My father was a good footballer; he played for Barkingside United and won several amateur caps for his native Wales. So he was my footballing idol as a young boy.

Growing up in the seventies, there were two teams that dominated the First Division: Liverpool and Leeds United. As my sister was a Leeds fan I inevitably become a Liverpool fan! I still have the pictures of me wearing the 1976 strip, which was the red crew-neck jersey with the white band around the neck. For me my favourite players were the greats of the team, such as Kenny Dalglish, Kevin Keegan, John Toshack and Ray Clemence. As my grandfather used to say, in those days football was about passion and the love of the game. Unfortunately, today it has been tainted slightly by the amount of money involved, which I think has restricted the level of raw talent like we saw in the game up to the early eighties. I have found memories of going to games with my grandfather wrapped in my red-and-white scarf, knitted by my grandmother, which was about six feet long, and being crammed into standing terraces spinning my wooden rattle around. There was nothing like the violence we see today and everyone was there to enjoy the game, win, lose or draw … it was a good day out for all the family.

CHERRY DEE

GLAMOUR MODEL

I love Liverpool because we are ace and my favourite player is Stevie Gerrard.

LEE DIXON

FORMER FOOTBALLER

My favourite team is Manchester City.

STEVE DIXON

TV SPORTS PRESENTER

My favourite football team as a youngster was Manchester United, mainly because at school in the north-west of England everyone either supported Manchester United or Liverpool!

Oddly enough, my fave player was not associated with Man U at all, but Spurs. Gary Mabbutt proved to be an inspiration when I was diagnosed as an insulin-dependent diabetic. Although it is a major blow to a young man and affects things like physical exercise, at least till you get used to it a little, Gary Mabbutt proved you could be a professional sportsman and diabetic. As a result, he was the footballer I most admired.

Since then, in my work as a journalist, I have met quite a few of the England team and they are an impressive bunch. The last time I met them was just before the World Cup 2006 when they all came to the new Wembley Stadium, which is one of the most impressive buildings I have ever seen. Although he has in many ways proved to be controversial and loved and unloved in equal measure, I have a great admiration and respect for David Beckham as both a player and a person. He always seems genuinely warm and gentle and meeting him is always a pleasure.

I hope that the book is a success.

MATTHEW DUQUENOY

ACTOR

I spent my teens abroad and didn't get any football coverage while I was there, so I never got into supporting and following the Premiership or any league here. Once I returned I decided not to jump onto any bandwagon (which would've been Manchester United) and just be the 'neutral supporter' - which gives me plenty of thrills but none of the tears, so it's nice and healthy (despite plenty of people saying I'm not a real footie fan cos I don't support a club team).

Watching the European games is great because I support all the English teams that play - even to the extent of wanting Blackburn to win. But if I had to pick a club team then I'd select Liverpool. They're clean, great to watch, great manager, great history and they have the best midfielder in the world - Steven Gerrard.

But if I had to choose 'A Team', 'My Team' - then it would be England.

NOEL EDMONDS

PRESENTER

My favourite football team is West Ham United.

GEORGE EGG
COMEDIAN

I suppose, if pressed, I'd have to say Charlton, since I was born there and I used to have a denim jacket with a 'Valley Rescue Squad' patch on the back until someone pointed out it was referring to Charlton FC, or maybe Crystal Palace, since they were my local team from the age of 2 and our neighbour used to be a ref there (he gave me a football signed by the team once for Christmas). But, to be honest, I really hate football and have never had the remotest interest in it at all.

My brother likes football enormously, and this year when the World Cup was on he asked me if I was going to watch that.

"No," I replied, "I hate football."

"But it's The World Cup," he said.

"I know," I replied, "but that's like me saying I hate mushrooms, and you saying, 'Yeah, but it's a really big one'"!

MICHAEL FENTON-STEVENS

ACTOR

My favourite football team is, and always has been, Manchester United. I am your typical London supporter. No real connection with Manchester (I was actually brought up a stone's throw from Millwall - as a consequence, our windows were often broken on a Saturday afternoon!)

My father introduced me to them in the early sixties. He loved them as he had seen the great pre-Munich side play, loved Bobby Charlton and Sir Matt, and he couldn't fail but pass that love on to me. It was purely anecdotal. He never took me to see them play; my Saturdays were spent playing wild goose chase on the empty Millwall terraces; but his devotion was such that I could not resist. My father bought our first television in 1968 (a tiny machine with a magnifying glass contraption on the front) so that we could watch the European Cup final. It was only recently that I discovered that they played in blue. For me they will always have light grey shirts in that game.

Although I of course adore Best (my father defended him when he stole Miss World's fur coat, by the way) and the mighty Cantona, my favourite has always been Steve Coppell. I even forgive him for the 1-1 draw with Reading during 2006/2007.

I now get to games whenever I can and my passion for them has never dimmed. The last 15 years have been great for us United supporters, but you must realise that I had to endure many years of failure and an entire school life where everyone else supported either Chelsea, Arsenal or the all-conquering Liverpool.

Best of luck with your endeavours.

PERRY FENWICK

ACTOR

I seriously am a 'proper' Eastender thru and thru, born in West Ham. There was never any say in the matter about who I would support. I still go and fortunes are still hiding!

For players, no doubt - Bobby Moore. If only players these days carried themselves, both on and off the pitch, the way Bob did the world would be a better place.

Good luck with the book.

JULIE FERNANDEZ

ACTRESS & PRESENTER

I am not a big football fan, except for when the World Cup is on every four years and of course I then support England. However, all the men in my life - my father, my brother and my boyfriend - are supporters of Tottenham.

My favourite players are from the 1990 World Cup: Gary Lineker and Paul Gascoigne.

SIR RANULPH FIENNES
EXPLORER

My only favourite football team is ENGLAND. David Beckham (and his amazing set-piece accuracy) remains my most impressed situation. A real skill.

SIR TOM FINNEY

FORMER FOOTBALL PLAYER

First of all, I am pleased that Chris is compiling this book and hope it raises plenty of money for charity.

My favourite team is Preston North End, because being a local boy I always wanted to play for them. I had a trial, and was told I was too small. My father was a very persistent person and I got a trial at a later date, and must have impressed as I was offered a place on the ground staff, to train as a professional footballer. I was over the moon about this, but my father, who had served as an apprentice plumber, was adamant that I finish my apprentiship as a plumber. I was disappointed as you can imagine. But, on second thoughts, it was the best advice I ever had.

I went on to play for Preston North End 'B' side in the local league, as an inside forward. I became an outside right by pure chance, because we were due to play Manchester United Juniors, and the outside right was injured. I was told to report and was informed I was playing outside right. I was astounded but would do my best. I must have done alright as I was told by the chairman of Preston North End that I should forget all about being an inside forward, and that is how I became an outside right. I spent all my professional career with Preston North End.

My favourite players were Stanley Matthews, Neil Franklin, Billy Wright, Tommy Docherty, Willie Cunningham, Charlie Wayman, Tommy Thompson, Jimmy Baxter and Stan Mortensen.

Preston were my favourite team because they played the ball on the ground, and were a great side to be with.

JAMES FISHER
ACTOR

I am a West Ham United supporter.

I have been a fan as long as I can remember, as a kid I had the West Ham duvet set, bin, light shade, the kits, sports bag, pencil sharpener - you name it, I had it!

My dad is a West Ham fan, so I probably got a little bit of encouragement from him, seeing as I'm the youngest of three brothers and the other two support Spurs and Chelsea - I guess I was his last chance!

Some of my early memories are of the 1980 FA Cup final win, the League Cup defeat, and players like Trevor Brooking and Alan Devonshire. I was a season ticket holder for some time, but nowadays I have to limit myself to trips to Upton Park when I'm not filming or have other commitments.

In recent times I think the best player I've seen at the Boleyn has to be Paolo Di Canio - passion ingrained into every molecule of his being, a top player and some great memories.

BRUCE FORSYTH, CBE
TV PRESENTER

Arsenal and Tottenham Hotspur - they're my favourites. My favourite players are Thierry Henry and Dennis Thompson.

I would like to wish you all the best for your fund-raising activities connected with The Willow Foundation.

MICHAEL FOSTER

MP

I am a lifelong Birmingham City fan, and true football supporters never change their team.

My favourite player has to be Trevor Francis, I witnessed his four goals in a match when he was sixteen (and I was a lot younger!)

BERNARD GALLAGHER

GOLFER

My favourite team is Fulham.

FENTON GEE

ACTOR & RECORDING ARTIST

My favourite team is Tottenham Hotspur.

I have supported them since I was a little nipper as they are local and my family follow them too.

My all-time favourite player is Gary Mabbutt.

I follow Spurs but don't get the time to go to White Hart Lane as much as I would like. My favourite recent players are Ledley King, Paul Robinson and Robbie Keane.

URI GELLER

MOTIVATIONAL & INSPIRATIONAL SPEAKER

Thanks for thinking about me. My favourite teams are Reading and Exeter, that's all I can say.

Good luck with your book. Much energy.

PHIL GIBBS

UNDERWORLD & BUSINESSMAN

My team is Chelsea and has been since 1968 when I saw my first match - Chelsea 4 QPR 0 (thank God QPR didn't win!) I'm not a jump on the bandwagon bloke. I used to go to both home and away games every week when I was younger (I was single then, so had a few quid!) I have seen Chelsea relegated three times but you have to stick with them; that's what supporting your team is about.

The best players ever to wear the blue shirt were Peter Osgood, God rest him, the king of Stamford Bridge and Franco Zola, a genius who played the game with a smile. Zola and Ossie were true greats of the game.

The greatest player I have ever seen, though, has to be George Best. I saw the great man play for Man Utd against Chelsea in 1973 and for Northern Ireland v. England in 1970. He was simply the best. What a privilege it was to have seen him play. Ossie and Bestie ... Rest In Peace.

SANDRA GIDLEY

MP

When I was about fourteen I used to support Arsenal, but that was more because I fancied Charlie George than having any great interest in football!

I now just support England!

JANEY GODLEY
ACTRESS & COMEDIENNE

My favourite team has always been Manchester United. I never wanted to be associated with a Scottish team as it smacked of sectarianism.

My favourite player of all time is George Best as he was so sexy, talented and gorgeous! I was lucky to meet him at a comedy gig in 2004 and spoke with him for over a hour and a half. I heard about him being an alcholic and wife beater and because I am Scottish and cynical I believed it. Well, I just took one look into his eyes that night and I thought 'I want to sleep with him!'

GRAHAM GOOCH
CRICKET COACH

My favourite all-time football team was the 1970 Brazilian team. A team of great individuals and fantastic skills, topped off by the incredible Pelé.

HOWARD GRIFFITHS

TV & RADIO PRESENTER

Without doubt my favourite football team always has been and still is Manchester United. Man U was the team for me throughout my school years, but when Ryan Giggs played his first Man U game against Everton in 1991 the club in my eyes became even more distinguished because of his Cardiff roots. I started my broadcast career back in 1991. My first report for the BBC was on board Concorde supersonic en route to New York reporting for the Radio 5 'Rave' programme presented by Rob Brydon. As far as I'm concerned Ryan Giggs' speed on the pitch is supersonic and we've all 'raved' about his legendary dribbling skills ever since he was first brought on as a substitute for Denis Irwin back in 1991.

A world-class team with a world-class player from Wales who shines on and off the pitch and is a superb ambassador for the many charities he supports. I was lucky enough to meet him in 2002 when Wales were playing Norway at the Millennium Stadium. My mate Kurt Nogan who was playing for Cardiff City at the time introduced me to Ryan at the after-game party. We chatted with the likes of Gary Speed and after half an hour I said to Ryan, "You're quite a shy guy." He said, "I am a bit." I thought, what an amazing individual. After all he's achieved, he remains down to earth and is an inspiration to all new young football talent being developed at grass-roots level.

PETER HAIN

MP

I have been a Chelsea fanatic since 1965 and have watched all the stars, like Peter Osgood, the most brilliant striker in British football and worldwide, especially in his heyday before he broke his leg. Stars like Charlie Cooke, who I have seen dribble from the halfway line to score a goal; Ray Wilkins scoring from the halfway line, and then the really tenacious characters like Ron 'Chopper' Harris through to the later stars like Kerry Dixon who scored a hat-full of goals for us. In the modern age, Gianfranco Zola has delighted us all with his magician-like qualities on the football pitch, while Ruud Gullit gave us power, precision and class. Now we have really fantastic players at Chelsea such at Didier Drogba and Frank Lampard, who has come on a treat since he first joined us to become a world-class midfielder. Together with John Terry, a towering defender, and of course the world's best goalkeeper in Peter Cech, we have a fantastic defence. So whether it has been through good times or bad times, I have always been somebody who has clung to the edge of his seat when watching Chelsea. I love getting to the stadium when ministerial duties permit, but more often these days I have to watch on TV. Either way, I am always cheering on the Blues with both my parents, my sons and my grandchildren.

MIKE HALLOWELL
COLUMNIST & AUTHOR

My favourite football team is Newcastle United. I was born and bred on the banks of the River Tyne, and being a Toon Army fan was taken as read. Occasionally we'd hear of a strange tribe a few miles further south that supported Sunderland. I'm not saying Sunderland weren't any good, but if we beat them by anything less than a fifteen-goal margin we'd shoot the manager and hold a wake.

I remember my first trip to St James's Park as a ten-year-old. We were playing Liverpool. This was back in the good old days when visiting supporters from 'the other side' could mingle with us and they'd be treated with courtesy and respect.

We got beat 2-0, and this huge Scouser gave me half of his meat pie and a cough drop by way of consolation. I've always had a soft spot for Liverpudlians since then, bless 'em.

Back in 1969, Bobby Moncur knocked in a brace and we won our first European title (and last major trophy), the Inter City Fairs Cup. Since then we've lived in hope.

My whole family is Black and White to the bone, except for my daughter-in-law. She's gorgeous and I love her to bits, but she's a Sunderland supporter. I've heard there's a clinic in Switzerland where she could get specialist treatment, but first she'll have to recognise she has a problem.

I had a drink with Toon Army legend Malcolm McDonald a couple of years back. He didn't look a day older than when he played for the Toon. I think he's found the secret of eternal youth, but he hasn't shared it with me yet. I'm still an ugly bastard. All together now … Howay the lads!

CHRISTINE HAMILTON

FAMOUS TV & RADIO GUEST

I obviously support England - or failing that one of the principalities - but that's as far as it gets. I can't give you an England favourite player - I love them all - when they're winning that is!

Good luck with your excellent project.

NEIL HAMILTON

FORMER MP

I used to support Swansea Town (now Swansea City) but that was when I was 12 and 13. I don't follow football now though.

AINSLEY HARRIET

CHEF

My favourite football team is Arsenal who I have supported all my life. I went to my first game in 1970 and still go with the gentlemen who took me all those moons ago.

In the early days I loved Georgie Armstrong and wanted to be Charlie George, but then came Liam Brady whom I idolised as he was pure class. When he left for Italy it took us years to rebuild. I'm absolutley thrilled that he is still associated with the youth development at our club.

Today's heroes can be here today and gone tomorrow. Ian Wright was the complete entertainer and a wonderful goalscorer who never gave the goalkeeper a chance to settle, always took the shot early and we all waited for some kind of celebration.

Dennis Bergkamp brought class and sophistication to the team and also some very special goals. Super captains in the form of Tony Adams and Patrick Vieira - the utter class of the ballet dancer of the football world.

Thierry Henry - how special, and more to come from a great team and a manager that the whole world loves.

Thank you Arsenal - I'm proud to be a fan!

GLENN HARROLD
AUTHOR

I am a big Chelsea fan and have supported them since the early seventies. I remember watching the 1970 cup final against Leeds on TV and becoming totally hooked. My family originate from South West London and Chelsea was our local team. My grandfather was a well-known bookie in the area. He would go to Chelsea one week and Fulham the next, as the two clubs would alternate their home and away fixtures in those days to attract more supporters.

As a lad I used to stand in the shed and experienced the highs and lows of watching them go up and down from the old 1st and 2nd divisions during the 1980s. Charlie Cooke was my favourite player from that era, and my mate and I once wrote a letter to the Scottish FA insisting he should play for Scotland. Surprisingly, we received a pleasant reply saying that they would consider our proposal!

I used to go to most home games and many away games in the late 1970s and 1980s. It was a rough and ready time. If the game was no good there was always the other entertainment on show: watching the rival supporters beat the hell out of each other. I remember being chased, getting caught up in crushes and feeling the excitement and anxiety when visiting grounds like the Den at Millwall. I once watched Chelsea at the Den whilst standing with the Millwall supporters as I went with a mate who was a Millwall fan. Fortunately Chelsea lost 3-0 as I was worried that if they scored I'd forget where I was and start cheering.

Supporting Chelsea during the '70s, '80s and well into the '90s were frustrating times as we never won anything other than the 2nd Division titles a few times. So the 1997 cup final was a watershed experience, as after the long hiatus CFC finally won a trophy. I was lucky enough to get two tickets and I was able to take my 10-year-old son to see the final against Middlesbrough. It was quite an emotional day for many of us diehards who had followed them for so long without seeing any success. My brother, myself and a few friends hired a stretch limo for the trip to Wembley and back. We played the Suggs song 'Chelsea Cheslea' at full volume all the way there and back. The limo driver was cool and let us indulge ourselves. That day was my best memory of supporting the Blues.

My brother is still a season ticket holder and I still go now and again. It's good to see them doing so well, although I do find it a bit clinical now and I kind of miss the old days. They were exciting and unpredictable.

GARY HAVELOCK

FORMER INTERNATIONAL SPEEDWAY RIDER

Football - it's one of my favourite subjects.

My favourite team is my local club Middlesbrough, and my favourite Boro player was the little Brazilian magician Juninho. The Boro squad at the moment is in a transitional period but we have a fantastic youth accademy; you just need to look at the local boys now starting in the first team. The likes of Downing, Cattermole, Morrisson, Taylor, etc., are coming along and I feel that in 3 to 5 years we will have a fabulous squad of mainly young local talent. It doesn't get much better that that.

My favourite other team is Barcelona. When on holiday as a kid in Spain with my parents they bought me a Barcelona kit and it was fabulous. I was the envy of every kid in my school when I came home.

NIGEL HAVERS

ACTOR

My favourite football team is Fulham. I have supported them for over 20 years.

My favourite player is Zat Knight.

JAMES HAWKINS

AUTHOR

I was at one time the head of the Transport Police in central East Anglia, so both Colchester United and Ipswich Town were on my patch, and I've been to many games - on duty. But that was a very long time ago.

Regarding national teams: I would have to say Canada (if we have a team!) Here in Canada, soccer - as it is called (football is that American game) - is really known as a girl's game. I'm sure there is a Canadian men's team, but they are probably 200th in the world.

STEPHEN HENDRY

SNOOKER PLAYER

My dad Gordon was a Jambo and still is to this day. We lived in Robertson Avenue (Edinburgh), which was about a ten-minute walk away from Tynecastle. So it was easy to support your team. And if I didn't behave myself he would take me back the following week as a punishment!

But then my dad opened up his fruit shops and we moved away. He worked on Saturdays, and if he couldn't go, I couldn't go. Then snooker took over my life, so going to the football has taken a very distant back seat.

But my elder son Blaine has gone to a couple of games with my dad, including the Scottish Cup final in 2006.

When I was a kid in the mid-'70s Bobby Prentice was my favourite player, and I'd be an outside left, just like him, any time I'd play. I'm never quite sure how good he was. All I do know is that there was a roar of expectation any time he got the ball.

While they might have ambitions to compete with them, Hearts are not Rangers or Celtic, so when they do win anything the fans savour the moment. So I think that anyone who has ever won a trophy with Hearts at any time is considered something of a hero - regardless of how ordinary they might have been the rest of the time.

SAM HEUSTON

MODEL & FORMER BIG BROTHER CONTESTANT

My favourite football teams are Chelsea, Manchester United and Real Madrid because all the players are fit!

SUE HOLDERNESS

ACTRESS

My favourite football team is Reading as they are my local team.

I think Steve Coppell is the BEST manager during Premiership years. Reading get better and better.

EAMONN HOLMES

TV PRESENTER

My favourite team is Manchester United. I have a lot of memories from working in Manchester and spending a lot of my youth there.

My favourite team player is Eric Cantona.

I wish you all the best with your book.

MICHAEL HOWARD

MP

The football teams I support are Liverpool, Swansea City and Folkestone.

I was born and grew up near Swansea and used to watch them as a boy. I still look out for their results and occasionally am able to watch them. Folkestone Invicta are my local team in Kent. They play in the Ryman Premier League and I watch them whenever I can.

But my real football passion is Liverpool, the team I have supported since I was a boy. I started supporting them because my favourite player in those days was Billy Liddle, who was an absolutely outstanding winger and whom I greatly admired. Since then I have had the pleasure of watching many great Liverpool teams - including the present one.

CHARLES INGRAM

FORMER BRITISH ARMY MAJOR & FAMOUS *WHO WANTS TO BE A MILLIONAIRE?* CONTESTANT

I have supported Leeds United through their ups and downs all my life, that's from 1963.

My favourite all-time Leeds United player is Billy Bremner. There are many others who must be mentioned, including Peter Lorimer, Norman Hunter, Jack Charlton, Allan Clarke, Johnny Giles, Eddie Gray, Paul Madeley, Gary McAllister, Gordon Strachan, Nigel Martyn, David Batty and even Eric Cantona and Rio Ferdinand before they left for Man United. They, and many more, are legends.

JOHN INVERDALE

TV SPORTS PRESENTER

My favourite team of all time would be the Spurs' cup-winning team of 1967 - the first football team I was able to recite by heart.

But while as the years went by and I had pictures of Alan Mullery and Martin Peters and the rest on my wall at home, my overriding memory of those days is a poster of Joe Royle that my dad inspected one night (he was a dentist) and he told me exactly what kind of work Joe needed doing to various front teeth. I went to interview him many years later. It was one of the more bizarre interviews I've done because we discussed fillings and not formations.

GLENDA JACKSON

MP

My birthplace was Birkenhead, so I claim to support Tranmere Rovers. I have never seen them play I might add!

Good luck with the book.

JIM JEFFRIES

COMEDIAN

My favourite football team is Fulham. My other favourite is the Austrialia national team.

My favourite player is the Australian Tim Cahill. Other favourites are Australians Craig Johnson and Mark Bosnich.

PAT JENNINGS

FORMER FOOTBALLER

My favourite football team is the North London team Tottenham Hotspur.

DEBI JONES

TV & RADIO PRESENTER

All I DO remember is working for BBC Radio Merseyside and doing the warm-up for a Derby game in Wembley around 1984/85. I did the warm-up, then decided to get the early train home and miss the match, as I really wasn't into football. I gave my ticket to an old fella who was sitting outside Wembley, and was going to listen to the match on the radio and just soak up the atmosphere. He couldn't believe his luck!

I met him again years later. He came up to me and said, "Remember me? You gave me the Wembley ticket for nothing?" I smiled at him. "I ended up in b***** prison!" he said. Evidently the ticket I gave him was a special press pass, and they thought he'd stolen it!

LYNNE JONES

MP

I support Aston Villa but only nominally. I only go to football matches occasionally. The sport I am most involved in is cycling.

BORIS JOHNSON

MP

My favourite football team is Newcastle, because my son Milo venerates them, especially Alan Shearer.

JUDGE JULES

DJ

My favourite team is Arsenal - I'm a season ticket holder at the Emirates Stadium (and formerly at Highbury).

My favourite player when I first started going as a young kid was Liam Brady, and my favourite player of recent times is Cesc Fabregas.

ALAN KENNEDY

FORMER FOOTBALLER

Having been born in the fifties I didn't get a chance to see much football on TV, so it was Newcastle United and Sunderland (my two local teams) that I used to go and watch. Sunderland was my first love because of a player called Charlie Hurley, a big, strapping centre half. Then I saw Bobby Charlton on TV scoring goals (spectacular ones) from all over the pitch. So I decided to follow Manchester United and England. He was my hero.

When I joined Newcastle United on the training staff in the late 1960s, players like Bob Moncur, Wyn Davies and Bryan (Pop) Robson were my heroes. However, when I had the chance to make my debut for Newcastle in 1973, two of these players had moved on and players like Malcolm Macdonald and Terry Hibbit came in to take their place.

I still think the Liverpool team of the late 1970s was the best club team.

Best of luck with the book.

BAP KENNEDY

SINGER

Speaking from my lofty perch as a celebrity … I'm not big on the beautiful game but I have a special place in my heart for the 1994 World Cup Republic of Ireland squad.

The 1-0 victory over Italy on 18 June was the greatest day in Irish football as far as I can recall. Jack Charlton was a god and Ray Houghton's genius goal in the 12th minute is the only football statistic I'll ever know.

All the best.

MOIRA KERR

SINGER & SONGWRITER

My favourite team is Scotland. My favourite player is Stephen Presley.

Good luck with the book.

RONNIE KNIGHT

UNDERWORLD FIGURE & AUTHOR

Football to me is entertainment and I have to be entertained when watching a match. The only teams that can do that these days are Chelsea and Manchester United so I watch them mostly.

The entertainers in the modern game are few and far between so seeing them in action is a rare treat.

Today, I would have to put Wayne Rooney at the top of my list. He's great to watch.

From yesteryear, there was nobody to touch George Best and Jimmy Greaves. What else can I say about those two?

LEE LATCHFORD EVANS

SINGER

My favourite football team and the team I was born into (you could say) is Everton FC.

You may notice my middle name - Latchford. This is not a double barrelled surname as some people think, it is actually my middle name and I was named after Bob Latchford, a very famous Everton player. So as you can imagine I was born with a blue scarf round my neck.

I used to go almost every Saturday, or whenever there was a home game, with my dad. I remember the days when there wasn't seating all around the club and us kids used to climb onto the railings around the pitch so we could see better. My dad used to put me on his shoulders and if the team scored I would almost always fall off with the sudden surge of the crowd's excitement at the goal.

My favourite players were Gary Lineker, Kevin Sheedy, Andy Gray and Pat van den Hauwe.

Kevin Sheedy was like the first Beckham - could bend a ball in from a free kick anywhere; Andy Gray would header the ball no matter how low it was, Gary Lineker was the gentleman's goal hanger, a pure talent in the box but I don't think I ever saw him booked; and Pat, or 'Psycho Pat' as the terrace used to call him, was a different kettle of fish - I think he forgot about the ball sometimes but the crowd loved him!

Well, I was brought up a true Blue and always will be, never forgetting the days with my father and the buzz of going to see my team on a Saturday afternoon.

Thanks and good luck with the book.

CARLTON LEACH
AUTHOR & SUBJECT OF MAJOR FILM

I was one of the original members of the ICF (Inter City Firm) with pals like Vic Dark and Cass Pennant, so obviously I am West Ham United through and through and always will be. I have been going to watch the Hammers since I was six years old. Later on, West Ham weren't that great so we made our own entertainment on the terraces!

We would travel all over the country and take on anyone on their own doorstep. The ICF became the most feared football firm of all.

On the pitch, I have had the honour of watching our World Cup winners Bobby Moore, Geoff Hurst and Martin Peters as well as Billy Bonds and Trevor Brooking. My number-one player of all time, though, has to be Paolo Di Canio. This may surprise some people, but that guy was class, a great player.

GARY LINEKER
FORMER FOOTBALL PLAYER

My favourite team is Leicester City.

I was born in Leicester and went to watch the Foxes with my father and grandfather from an early age.

My favourite players were Frank Worthington and Peter Shilton.

Good luck with the book.

DOUG LIVERMORE

FORMER FOOTBALL PLAYER

The first team I supported as a young boy was Everton and my favourite player was Alex Young.

I signed for Liverpool FC when I was aged 17 years 11 months and my favourite player at that time was Ian St John.

I hope you raise a lot of funds for this very worthy cause.

ROGER LLOYD PACK

ACTOR

My favourite football team is Tottenham Hotspur; I support them because my father did, even though we used to live a stone's throw from Stamford Bridge. I am old enough to remember the great double team of the sixties (our long ago glory years).

My favourite player from that time was Jimmy Greaves.

NORMAN LOVETT

ACTOR & COMEDIAN

I am an Ipswich Town supporter that loves Arsenal and my top old player is Kevin Beattie and my current player would have to be Thierry Henry. My boyhood heroes were Law, Charlton, Best and Edwards.

I played football for my school and captained the side in my last year there. I played local football until I was 30, when it became much harder not so much because of my age but more to do with discovering lager. I did have one or two minor injuries and my knee joints are a bit creaky, but I would not have changed anything because it's the greatest game as far as I'm concerned. When someone asks me how a gig went I always draw on football to answer them: "I won two nil." "It was a tough draw." "I got a hat-trick."

I used to watch Ipswich when Bobby Robson managed them and it was a good time for them as they won the FA Cup and the UEFA Cup with his teams. He also was the first manager to bring in players from Europe with the Dutch player Arnold Mühren being one of my favourites. I don't think Ipswich Town will ever rise to those heights again but I live in hope.

JIM MAGILTON

FOOTBALL MANAGER

In answer of your questions:

* My boyhood club were Celtic.
* Kenny Dalglish was one of my favourite players.

JASON MARRINER

FAMOUS FOOTBALL HOOLIGAN & AUTHOR

My favourite football team is Chelsea. My dad supported them so I followed them from the day dot. I also like Glasgow Rangers.

The best matches are any time when the boys (Chelsea) beat Tottenham or when Rangers beat Celtic.

My favourite players were Peter Osgood, Kerry Dixon, Kevin Keegan and Paul Gascoigne. Gazza was the best player that I ever saw live.

MICHAEL MARSHALL SMITH

AUTHOR

England - they didn't really get it together for the 2006 World Cup, for a variety of reasons - not that we missed much - but usually we make sure we endure the emotional ups and downs in a pub full of like-minded folk. At one of the ups in Euro 2004 this included some huge guy I'd never met before getting so excited that he grabbed me around the shoulders from behind and shook me up and down - sending the contents of my pint over everyone in sight. My favourite competition would have to be Euro 96: I can remember watching England v. Holland with our neighbours and all of us looking at each other in frank disbelief as the national side, for once, looked like they might be a bit tasty; and, finally, watching England v. Germany in a pub absolutely stuffed full of Austrians, and walking down the street in Islington afterwards to see grown men sitting on the pavement outside pubs sobbing their hearts out.

GRAHAM MASTERTON

AUTHOR

I'm a Gooner. My favourite team is Arsenal. They have been a team in transition since the 'boring old Arsenal' days. Under the influence of manager Arsene Wenger they have had two seasons winning the double and were finalists in the Champions League in 2005.

My favourite player is Thierry Henry, whose pace is uncatchable, and whose loyalty to Arsenal is even more intense than previous captains like Patrick Vieira. Thierry is leading a young team in a new stadium with outstandingly fair play and dedicated teamwork.

BILL MAYNARD

ACTOR

My favourite team is Leicester City, especially when Frank Worthington played.

I played for the 'A' team when I was 15.

My other favourite player was Septimus 'Sept' Smith who played for Leicester City between 1929 and 1949.

BRIAN MILTON

JOURNALIST & ADVENTURER

When I was a boy my favourite football team was Blackpool, and my hero then was Stanley Matthews. Now my favourite team is Reading, because they got to the Premiership on their own resources and without expensive foreigners, and they're staying there for the same reason.

It's rugby teams I follow now, rather than football. In my opinion, it was Martin Johnson who was primarily responsible for England winning the Rugby World Cup, and without him we would not have won it.

SHAZIA MIRZA

ACTOR & COMEDIENNE

My favourite team is Aston Villa because all my brothers supported them and I grew up in Birmingham so it was close to our house and we always used to go there on a Saturday.

My favourite player is Chris Sutton.

My favourite footballing hero is David Beckham, always dignified throughout his career, versatile, and has adapted himself to all situations all over the world. He really is a footballing hero and is always entertaining.

SOPHIE MOLETA

SINGER & SONGWRITER

My favourite team is The Squids (Island Bay Wellington, New Zealand).

My favourite player is Te-Atawhai Maginness.

KEVIN MORAN

FORMER FOOTBALLER

My team was Liverpool FC.

Manchester United had already been picked by another brother and the rule was that we all had different teams to support. Liverpool were very successful at the time so it was an easy choice.

My favourite player was Roger Hunt.

PIERS MORGAN

FORMER EDITOR OF *THE NEWS OF THE WORLD* & *THE MIRROR*

My favourite football team is Arsenal. I've had a season ticket for 12 years, and supported them since I was six, when we won the double in 1971. My favourite players have been Charlie George, Liam Brady, Ian Wright, Dennis Bergkamp, Freddie Ljungberg and Thierry Henry. And my least favourite was Pascal Cygan!

My all-time Arsenal XI would be: Seaman, Dixon, Adams, Keown, Winterburn, Vieira, Brady, Bergkamp, Ljungberg, Wright and Henry.

NEIL MULLARKEY

ACTOR

My favourite team is Manchester United.

I saw a picture of Nobby Stiles in 1967; a cigarette card probably. Red is my favourite colour so I liked the look of him. The next year, I was allowed to stay up (in my pyjamas) and watch the first football match I had ever seen on TV (or anywhere, in fact. I lived in France prior to 1967 and my dad didn't like football. He preferred rugby). Manchester United won the European Cup. Nobby was my favourite. I liked his style, his smile, his teeth (or lack thereof) and his thick glasses.

BRIAN MURPHY

ACTOR

My earliest memories of attending a football league game was back in the late '40s, Charlton and Millwall. My favourite players then were the goalkeepers: Sam Bartram for Charlton, an acrobatic keeper who I tried to emulate when I took to play the game; and Millwall's keeper Bumstead, who was forever chewing gum which he took out and stuck on the goalpost before making a save.

My original hometown was Portsmouth and whenever possible I watched them when they played London teams or when I visited my parents living in Portsmouth.

When I played the tabletop football game 'Subbuteo' my side was Pompey and the stars of the team were the two wingers, Harris and Froggart. Two of the real greats that I think would outclass our present top players were Stanley Matthews and Tommy Lawton.

ANDY MURRAY

TENNIS PLAYER

My favourite team is FC Barcelona. My favourite player is Ronaldinho.

LIZ McCLARNON

SINGER

It is no secret that I am the BIGGEST Everton fan, and my favourite player is Tim Cahill.

I met Howard Kendall the other day and I was absolutely made up, but my favourite manager of all time is Joe Royle, and my childhood hero was Tony Cottee, BUT I think it goes without saying that I would have loved, loved, LOVED to have witnessed the great Dixie Dean playing!

FRANK McLINTOCK

FORMER FOOTBALLER

My favourite team are the Scottish giants Glasgow Celtic.

PAUL NUGENT

ACTOR

My favourite team are Manchester United - I've been a supporter for 20 years now (almost exactly the same as Alex Ferguson's reign). There were three main reasons I started supporting them as a kid in Dublin:

1. One day, I was given a football sticker album and loved the sound of their nickname, 'The Red Devils'.
2. Shortly after, I was changing around my room and in taking down a poster I'd got in some magazine of the pop band 'A-Ha', I discovered on the reverse was a poster of the 85/86 United squad, so I stuck it up on my wall that way instead.
3. And most importantly, a little later, I was hanging around with my three best pals, from whom I always had to be different. They were all Liverpool supporters and I remember them going on about Pool's run of Milk Cup wins, and I turned around and started arguing, saying I was a Man U fan.

After that, watching them play with their flamboyant style and learning their history, about the Munich disaster particularly, I was soon hooked and still am.

As for a favourite player, Giggs, Keane and Hughes come close, but at the top has to be Eric Cantona. He had huge arrogance, but the skill to back it up. Until Eric, I had never seen a flick that could break a defence. He embodied what United are all about - ambition, beauty and fire.

All the best with the project. I hope you raise plenty of money for what seems to be an excellent charity.

LEE OTWAY

ACTOR

My favourite team are Leeds United. The reason why I like them is because I am a Yorkshire lad and when I was growing up the Leeds team of the early '90s won the league.

My favourite players were from that team, i.e. Mel Sterland, Lee Chapman and David Batty. My favourite recent player is Gary Kelly because he is Leeds through and through.

My favourite national team are England and my favourite player was David Beckham even though he once played for Manchester United, because no one can pass a ball like Beckham can and he always got the important goals.

WES PACKER

COMEDIAN

I am a Cardiff City fan.

Best of luck with the book!

HAMBI PAPPAS

ACTOR

I am a Gooner and have been since I was a boy. The first time I ever went to church (Highbury) I witnessed my boyhood hero Ian Wright score his one-hundredth goal for Arsenal. I can play it back in my head like it was yesterday. He went up for a header from a cross and smashed it in home. I went nuts! I'd never cheered so loud in my life; I lost my voice. It was against his former club Crystal Palace. We went on to lose 2-1 but I wasn't upset. From that day I knew I was hooked. I then became a junior Gunner and went to home games religiously. Then we won the double with Wenger. That parade will go down as one of the best days of my life. Then quite a few years later my mother became a dental nurse to the Gunners - you can imagine my reaction to that! GO ON YOU GUNNERS!

I could go on about Arsenal for hours.

ALAN PARDEW

FOOTBALL MANAGER

My favourite team as a boy were Chelsea. My favourite player was Johan Cruyff.

I wish you every success in your efforts.

NICHOLAS PARSONS

TV PRESENTER & ACTOR

My favourite football team is Leicester City.

I once appeared on a quiz with two of their players as a guest celebrity. I watch mainly rugby and cricket, but after appearing on the quiz I adopted the Foxes (Leicester City) as my favourite club.

BILL PATERSON

ACTOR

It's decades since I had any interest in club football, and I only come alive when Scotland plays - usually tragically - in World Cups, etc.

My childhood heroes probably are long dead. So let's just say that Scotland and its struggles are the beginning and end of my football devotion and Dennis Law was and still is my footballing hero. I met him a while ago and he didn't disappoint - claimed I was a "number one actor", so who else can I vote for?!

CASS PENNANT
BEST-SELLING AUTHOR

My favourite team are West Ham United. Why? Simple - the club are its loyal fans; they're proper quality and no mugs.

My favourite players: Trevor Brooking really could put a ball on a sixpence and at his best I really did believe he walked on water. Alan Devonshire was a special player when you look at the route he took to get in the game. More recently, it has to be Paolo Di Canio, whose skill took your breath away. My all-time favourite player is the brilliant George Best, who was a tough player in a way that shames many a star striker today.

MICHAEL PERHAM

THE YOUNGEST PERSON EVER TO SAIL SINGLE-HANDED ACROSS THE ATLANTIC OCEAN

My favourite team are Arsenal and my favourite all-time player is Thierry Henry.

MARTIN PETERS

FORMER FOOTBALLER & MEMBER OF ENGLAND'S 1966 WORLD CUP WINNING TEAM

My favourite team have to be England's World Cup winning team of 1966, which I was a part of.

STEVEN PIRIE

AUTHOR

I am an avid Evertonian - season ticket holder for 25 years, dragged along by the ear by my father before that. It takes a certain personality to follow Everton - childlike optimism coupled with the daunting feeling of forever the underdog; you'll not find more loyal supporters than us Blues.

My favourite Everton team have to be the successful team of the mid-eighties, simply because they were a team that took us to the giddy heights of actually winning things. Exciting days, they were and, no matter what, there was always the feeling that the team would win each game, as if they were always good enough to recover if a goal was conceded and a game seemed lost.

Alas, the team were allowed to disband far too quickly, and the aftermath of Heysel, the European ban, was felt far more keenly at Goodison than elsewhere I think.

Favourite players? I must admit to liking the players of yesteryear more than today's bunch. There seemed always to be more characters around back then than there are today. I loved Neville Southall, the scruffiest millionaire on the block yet the best goalkeeper in the world, and sadly destined never to grace the World Cup finals. I loved the uncompromising tackling of Peter Reid; how he'd picked himself up and swear at the ref, and those being more sensible times, the ref would just smirk and swear back at him. I loved it that whenever Andy Gray attacked the ball he did so with total disregard for personal health, and woe betide the keeper in his way, too.

Love or loathe the likes of Eric Cantona, with his unfathomable ramblings and his Gallic nose in the air, you have to admire his genius with the ball. I've always wondered how Ian Rush (and later Robbie Fowler) always managed to score against us, even if he was having a clunker of a game. I recall once, at an away game, that referee George Courtney was warming up pre-game along the touchline and an Everton fan shouted, "Have a good game, Mr Courtney", and Courtney smiled and answered, "I'll do my best". Is it just me, or is it hard to think such an exchange would take place today, let alone the referee being addressed as 'Mr'?

PETER POLYCARPOU
ACTOR

I have always been a Spurs supporter though many of my friends are Gooners and indeed I was brought up just up the road from the old Gunners stadium.

I used to go to White Hart Lane regularly, but since the routine of Saturday afternoon matinees and a busy career have been my lot in life I am sadly unable to go as much as I would wish. My brother is a season ticket holder and whenever he or his wife or a friend doesn't use their ticket, and I'm free and there is an 'r' in the month, I go. The side I remember most seeing and admiring (though they certainly weren't the best side who played during that time but to me they played wonderful, elegant football) were around in the 1981/1982 season under Keith Burkinshaw and in which Ricki Villa and Ossie Ardiles played.

The memory of the goal at Wembley that Villa scored will live forever, not least because of its technical brilliance but also for its coming when it did to kill off any chance of a comeback after the Crooks equaliser. I believe it was also awarded the Wembley goal of the century in 2001. Villa had been substituted in the first match and then scored two goals in the replay!

The 100th Wembley Cup final replay was probably the best match I remember them playing, and winning that match was the icing on the cake, though Manchester City had a great side too. We even won the year after against Queens Park Rangers (Venables, ex-Spurs man too).

Steve Archibald, Garth Crooks, Glenn Hoddle and Steve Perryman stick out as being amongst my favourite players, and Pat Jennings was a fabulous goalkeeper who I don't think has been bettered at Spurs, even by Robinson. Alan Mullery, Martin Chivers and Alan Gilzean are also favourites. And, of course, Jimmy Greaves gets a mention as one of the great Spurs players.

It was fun remembering.

MARTIN POPPLEWELL

BROADCASTER & JOURNALIST

I'm not actually a hugh football fan but when the World Cup comes round I get hugely patriotic in support of England.

In terms of players, Michael Owen always comes across as a really lovely person - completely unaffected by his talent and success, and that's always an appealing quality in anyone.

Good luck with the book.

MICK QUINN

FORMER FOOTBALLER

My favourite team is Liverpool. Being brought up in Liverpool I used to go to the boys' pen at Anfield (under 15), then the Kop as a supporter.

The great teams were of the late 1970s and 1980s, and my favourite players were Kevin Keegan and Kenny Dalglish.

ALAN RAYMENT

DISABLED FUND-RAISER AND 2004 OLYMPIC TORCH-BEARER

I have supported Manchester United FC from the age of 10 after watching the FA Cup final when Norman Whiteside scored the winning goal. I first went to watch United when I was 12 years old and used to sit in the Stretford End.

I have been a wheelchair user for the last nine years and I am now a part of Manchester United Disabled Supporters (MUDSA). I get to as many games as I can, and usually attend between 15 and 30 games a season home and away. Old Trafford have the best facilities in the Premiership and I have not seen any better in Europe for disabled people - the view you get is amazing, especially in the new quadrants.

I must say that going to the away games is such a buzz - the Manchester United fans give the team some fantastic away support, the best in the world; the fans don't stop singing. I go to the away games with my mates; some of them have not missed a game in years - that's total dedication and they are a great bunch of lads. London away games are entertaining; trying to get on and off the underground is a nightmare for me. There are only two Premiership grounds I have not visited and they are Spurs and Watford. I have so many great stories to tell. Following United is great - every day out leads to a story, especially when we've travelled down to Cardiff a few times.

I have watched United in Europe, although I missed the 1999 European Cup win as I had just come out of hospital. I have been lucky enough to watch United in Spain, Germany and Prague and I went up to Rangers. We spend a few days at our destination, not doing much sightseeing though. I have so many stories: I punctured my tyres in Germany; in La Coruna I had to sit on a 6-foot fence so I could see the game; and at Stuttgart it was the beer festival - what a few days that was! When we went to Madrid we had an amazing journey, and the four days we spent there were brilliant. I was sat in the Madrid end and the atmosphere was electric.

I have been very lucky over the past few years to meet the Manchester United players. In 2001 and 2002 I met David Beckham, Roy Keane, Gary

Neville and rest of the squad. I have attended some MUDSA functions and I have met Sir Alex, Norman Whiteside, Lou Macari, Arthur Albiston, Alex Stepney and Lee Martin. In 2005 I met Wayne Rooney, Rio Ferdinand, Alan Smith and Paul Scholes. To meet the squad is unbelievable; they are so down to earth.

I am a keen fund-raiser. I do triathlons and 10k events in my wheelchair and in 2004 I completed the London Marathon. Manchester United FC have supported me with my fund-raising and I have written a few articles for the 'Rollin Reds' magazine on my events and when I hand-cycled over Vietnam and Cambodia.

My favourite players are:

- Bryan Robson. He was a brilliant player and he contributed 100% every time he played. Bryan would put his head where other players would not put their boot.

- Eric Cantona. We stole from our arch-rivals and he was the player that helped us win so many trophies. He had attitude, he was class and he scored some vital goals for United. I wish he hadn't retired when he did.

- Roy Keane. What a football player and leader he was. I met Keano a few times and he was a gentleman. He killed off Inter Milan in 1999 on our way to the treble. Keano was a class midfielder, rough, tough, and you just couldn't get past him.

- Rio Ferdinand. He is world class. Not much gets past Rio and just lately he has scored some cracking goals. Rio and Vidic work well together - they are turning out to be like Bruce and Pallister.

- Gary Lineker. He was class for England. You just knew when he got the ball it was going in the back of the net. He was the best striker England have ever had.

- Zinedine Zidane. To watch him play was breathless; he could run a midfield, and his football skills were incredible. I would have loved for him to come to United.

STEVE REDGRAVE, CBE

ROWER & FIVE TIMES OLYMPIC GOLD MEDALLIST

My favourite team is Chelsea. I have been a supporter since the late 1960s.

My all-time favourite player is Peter Bonetti ('The Cat') as I always wanted to be a goalkeeper. I only got as far as being the reserve team goalkeeper for my school team!

NICK REVELL

COMEDIAN

Growing up in a rugby league area, I never really followed a football team when I was a kid. I used to watch Leeds United in the early seventies from time to time, but it was never nearly as exciting as watching Featherstone Rangers. I never really cared who won, to tell you the truth, except in one game in about 1972 when a bunch of us skived off school to go to watch Wolves for the last game of the season. It was an evening kick-off. I think Leeds needed one point to clinch the league title. There were Aston Villa fans too, shouting for Leeds because, well, Wolves were local rivals. Villa weren't even in the First Division then, and I understood the difference between being interested in football and being a fan. It was a great atmosphere, really tense: intense. Leeds lost, 2-1 I think. Fantastic match - although I couldn't tell you anything about the quality of the football. But I probably didn't go to another game for eight or nine years after that.

When I moved to London I decided I'd have to adopt a team. No rugby was within reach at that time. Arsenal was out as my father is a Gunners fan, and we all know the song. So I opted for West Ham United - simply because of their tradition of always trying to play good football. Besides, who can fail to be impressed by 'Bubbles' - a team anthem that expresses such profound stoical resilience to the vagaries of fate in such a populist way? Zeno, Seneca, Marcus Aurelius - they'd have all definitely been Hammers fans for this reason alone.

I wouldn't have the audacity to claim to be a proper fan - I don't go often enough, and to claim I was a fan would be an insult to the real ones. But they're definitely my team.

My favourite player? Alan Devonshire. Even after the terrible leg break, he was so elegant - one of those players who manages always to create time and space on the ball. You can't help wondering what he would have become but for that injury.

It would also have been Paolo Di Canio. Every time I saw him play, he would do something - be it great or tiny, game changing or merely cheeky, that was just brilliant and worth the ticket on its own. However, by his own admission, he's a fascist, and I can't forgive him for that. Hardly logical to stop liking a brilliant athlete just because you don't agree with the politics, I suppose. Or hate his politics. But since when has there been anything logical about watching football?

MATTHEW REYNOLDS

ACTOR

I support Tottenham Hotspur despite all my family supporting Arsenal. I was born near Dalston, pretty much halfway between the two clubs' grounds. Maybe I went through a teen rebellion as a six-year-old, or maybe I was just bloody minded. Most likely, I simply enjoyed the way that the Spurs side played.

One of the family favourites is to drag out a photo of me holding the FA cup in the Arsenal shop in 1979 (I was only 5; I didn't know any better).

I had a season ticket on the Paxton Road during the late 1990s and early 2000s but gave it up when I moved to Rome.

As a boy, I loved Glenn Hoddle, Garth Crooks, Steve Archibald and Ossie Ardiles but still found myself wanting to be Kenny Dalglish when I was playing in the schoolyard.

May I wish you the best of luck with the book.

GEMMA SCOTT

TV PRESENTER

My favourite football team would have to be Blackburn Rovers Ladies Team (if only they would redesign their team colours to pink though!)

My reason for this is that I consider my life worth living, and if I picked any team outside of Blackburn Rovers my husband-to-be would never marry me - so the Ladies get my vote (and at least the blue of Chelsea is apparent in their current kit!)

My favourite men's team ... I was brought up on Chelsea so it would have to the boys in blue ... and player Andriy Shevchenko is very easy on the eyes! Otherwise it would be Engand and I never could resist Michael Owen either!

ROY 'PRETTY BOY' SHAW

UNDERWORLD, UNLICENSED AND BARE-KNUCKLE FIGHTING LEGEND & AUTHOR

I am an Eastender, a cockney through and through, so my football team are West Ham United. West Ham are a true East End team but their support is also extremely strong throughout Essex. My good pal Vic Dark is also a West Ham man; they have some good men supporting them.

I am also an extremely patriotic and proud England supporter, so my favourite players of all time are Bobby Moore, Geoff Hurst and Martin Peters - what great players they were. As we all know, the West Ham boys won the World Cup for England in 1966 (Bobby Moore was captain, Geoff Hurst scored a hat-trick and Martin Peters scored England's second goal). I had the great honour of knowing Bobby Moore and along with the whole country I was extremely upset when he passed away.

So my team were, are and always will be the Hammers.

JIM SMITH

FOOTBALL MANAGER

Although I started my career at Sheffield United, Sheffield Wednesday were my favourite team as they were the first team I ever saw play.

My favourite player in those days was Albert Quicksall.

NOEL 'RAZOR' SMITH

UNDERWORLD & AUTHOR

Growing up in South West London I was always a Chelsea fan, though the estate I lived on was bang in the centre of a football triangle that included Millwall in the east and Crystal Palace in the south. The nearest team, geographically, were Crystal Palace but, and no offence to Palace fans, they were a bit of a nonentity in footballing terms. They didn't have any memorable players and their hooligan crew were a bunch of clowns who couldn't knock the skin off a rice pudding. And, back in the early 1970s, for the working-class kids from inner-city estates, the game was as much about your reputation in a punch-up as it was about your team's position on the league tables. Millwall had a good crew - The F Troop - but the team were no great shakes on the pitch even then. Of the three teams around the manor, only Chelsea had it all: great individual football players and a hooligan element - The Shed Boot Boys - who had a terrifying reputation for violence and mayhem. Not only that, but 'Blue is the Colour' still knocks seven shades of shit out of 'I'm Forever Blowing Bubbles'! No, for me, Chelsea were always the team, and still are.

Now, a few people reading this, probably the Man U cans who live in Surrey, will be pointing out that Chelsea are a West London team and I'm a South London boy. I can see them now with smug smiles on their faces, feeling vindicated about their own lack of loyalty to their local sides, but I would just like to point out that the London Borough of Chelsea actually has a South West 1 postcode. So I class Chelsea as a South London team, and you can argue that one until you're blue (and white) in the face, but what can't speak can't lie.

The Chelsea team that I was weaned on contained such legendary players as Peter Osgood, Chopper Harris, Gary Locke, Alan Hudson, Johnny Hollins, Charlie Cooke and Peter 'The Cat' Bonnetti, amongst many others, and when I was a kid these men were like gods. But as I grew into my teens and discovered crime, girls and music (in that order), I drifted away from the football scene altogether. I still kept an eye on The Blues via the sports pages and the odd match on television, usually watched in a prison association room surrounded by various murderous rival fans of every team in the country! And, in prison, football really can be a matter of life and death, which is why most prisons won't allow the cons to wear any clothing with a team insignia on it; there have been a few deaths in jail down to football over the years. The tribal aspect of football followers becomes vastly magnified behind the walls of a prison, and if you really want to test your bottle there's nothing like being the only Chelsea fan in Walton Jail when The Blues are playing the Scousers in a cup final, or even a league match! Football is a serious business, and no more so than in jail.

It's hard to pick out one Chelsea player as a favourite amongst all the others. In today's game, which I started to follow seriously again around seven years ago, the names of Lampard, Terry and Droghba leap out of the fray, but there are so many others. In recent years Zola, Hasselbaink and Gudjonsen also stand out for me. But from my own personal golden era I would have to name Peter Osgood, The King of Stamford Bridge. When I was a kid I thought Peter Osgood was the coolest captain on the planet. And guess what? I wasn't wrong.

SUE SMITH

LADIES ENGLAND INTERNATIONAL FOOTBALLER

My favourite team are Everton. It's Everton because of my dad; he supports them and I just followed him as a child.

My favourite player is Ryan Giggs. He is a left winger like myself and is a flare player and always entertaining to watch. Also David Beckham for his attitude and comitment towards playing and training; he is always the last one out practising, etc.

TERRY SMITH

UNDERWORLD & AUTHOR

Ashamedly, my first memory of actually consciously supporting a professional football team must be when I was at Star Lane Primary School in East London when Chelsea were to face the near invincible Leeds United team in the FA Cup in the early 1970s. I recall the first black-and-white televised match at Wembley was a draw and Chopper Harris, Alan Hutchinson, Peter Osgood, et al., went on to win the midweek replay. Henceforth football became a significant part of my life.

But it was not long before the all-pervasive cultural tradition of following your local team compelled me to toe the line and support and worship the Clark Kents of Upton Park, the magnificent and frequently enigmatic West Ham United.

However, just as our glorious football anthem proclaims in 'I am Forever Blowing Bubbles,' '... like our dreams they fade and die.' West Ham appear to rise majestically to the dizzy heights of fame and fortune and then, more often than not, narrowly succumb to defeat whereupon deeply rooted frustration and despair become the norm.

I believe the litmus test of being a true football fan is when your team wins or loses, as it automatically dictates how you feel. In my case, when West Ham win a game I cannot wait to buy the following day's newspaper to read about 'my team's' marvellous victory. When they lose, however, it has an immediate effect on my disposition and I am one unhappy cat. Admittedly this is all part of being a time-honoured football fan.

On a more positive note, however, there are days in your life that remain forever ingrained in your memory, and one of those days was at the recent Championship play-offs at the Millennium Stadium in Cardiff when West Ham beat Preston Town 1-0 (Zamora) to regain entry into the Premiership League. I attended that game and I would slay a thousand dragons to experience such a wonderful full-blown technicolour day again. To see and witness so many joyous and ecstatic West Ham fans revel in the glory of victory was truly spiritual and uplifting. Some say that football has become a religion, with its cathedral-like stadiums, universal chanting and demi-gods on the pitch. I am addicted like most of us, but one word of warning, please don't talk to me if the mighty Hammers lose.

When it comes to selecting a great player from the past there are two ex-West Ham players that come to mind. First is the terrific unsung hero of Upton Park, Alan Devonshire. I watched him play for the Hammers in the 1980s and, although he was frequently compared to the eminently graceful Sir Trevor Brooking, I believe Alan was by far the better player.

He used to drift past opponents in the middle of the park as if he were a ghost. He would shimmy this way, that way, with such delicate balance and poise that before the opponents noticed he was gone and laying the ball off to his wingers or the strikers.

Having said that, however, my favourite player, whom I modelled myself upon when I was playing football, was the legendary Billy Bonds; a veritable colossus of a man who rolled down his socks and rolled up his sleeves and led his players into battle with all the grit and determination of an intrepid warrior.

Admittedly Billy was not the most skilful player in the world, but there are players that are born leaders that instinctively lift other players and in some respects police them, in as much as if they do not raise their game woe betide them when they return to the dressing room. Nonetheless, Billy was more than just a swashbuckling centre back. He was an incredible athlete. He trained like a Trojan and always came first in the pre-season cross-country race. He was valued so highly by those in power at Upton Park that he played first team football up to the marvellous age of 41 years. At the height of his illustrious career, he was earning a mere £600 per week. Compare this with the prima donnas of today that take home between £50,000 to £100,000 per week and it makes you wonder how much Billy Bonds would be worth in his prime today.

On a personal note, another reason why I vote Billy Bonds as my player of the century is because while I was serving 16 years for armed robbery in Britain's toughest jails I came up with an idea to write to Billy Bonds - who was the Hammers manager at the time in 1990 - and ask him if he would allow my sons to become match day mascots as I was unable to fulfil my parental duties and apply in person. He could have binned my letter or fobbed me off with some lame excuse or other, or ignored the missive entirely. But no, Billy passed the letter on to his understudy Brian Storey who arranged a match day tour of Upton Park where my sons were shown around the ground and dressing rooms and had photos taken with the manager. On that memorable day the Hammers thrashed Hull City 6-1. The photographs are reproduced in my best-selling autobiography *The Art of Armed Robbery*. So Mr Bonds has revealed himself not only as one of the great oaks of British football but also as a real and compassionate person who has time for those that are less fortunate that himself in the hour of need. For that reason, the great Billy Bonds remains my favourite player of all time.

DJ SPOONY

DJ

My favourite team is Liverpool.

RON STIRLING

ACTOR

I do not follow football at all in my adult life, although I did attend many matches with my dad when I was younger.

Laugh if you must, but our (my dad and I) team of choice was Partick Thistle. The match that stands out the most from memory was when Partick Thistle played Clyde on 28 February 1983 (I was nine-and-a-half years old). It was an amazing match, which we won 6-0, Mo Johnston scoring an incredible three of those goals. My dad was throwing me up and down so much, he almost threw me into orbit he was so excited! I kept the programme from that match for many years afterwards.

JAMES STONE

SINGER & SONGWRITER

Because I come from Liverpool I have always been interested in Liverpool Football Club. I admired Kevin Keegan as a footballer and was lucky enough to meet him at a charity function a few years ago.

I was never fortunate enough to see a match at Anfield when I was younger, but as fate would have it I have actually played at the club, latterly in 2006. The artists change in one of the boxes and we look out onto the pitch. It is kind of spooky, at night in the dark, but you still get the atmosphere.

My hero in football has to be Pelé, the most well-known footballer in the world. I don't think we have seen anyone to match his talent in any club worldwide, although there have been some exciting players coming through Anfield's gates over the years.

I wish you all the very best with your book Chris.

GRAHAM TAYLOR

FOOTBALL MANAGER

My favourite football team is Scunthorpe United. Why? Well it is my home town and 'The Iron' are the only team I have ever supported - in other words stood on the terraces, followed to away games, etc.; all my other clubs I have either played for or managed.

My parents moved to Scunthorpe in 1946. United were then a non-league team playing in the Midland League. By the fifties they were in the old Third Division North and come the end of that decade they had reached the old Second Division, missing out on promotion to the First Division to Bill Shankly's Liverpool!

Now those were the days!! My heroes? Jack Haigh and Jackie Brownsword. If you don't know them then you don't know your football! Jack Haigh was an inside forward of craft and cunning. Today he would be described as a midfield genius and would be a regular in the England team. He could see and make a pass that no other player could see or make. Believe me!

Jackie Brownsword was a left back who must have played 2,000 games for Scunthorpe. He was never injured. He was lightning quick and was a magnificient penalty taker, always putting the penalty to the right-hand side of the goalkeeper. He was the second fullback in the history of the game to score over 50 goals. His first 49 were from penalties and his 50th from open play in a Second Division game against Southampton. Terry Paine was the Saints' outside right (remember wingers!). He never got a kick against Jackie. Neither did the great Stanley Matthews in an FA Cup game in which Scunthorpe beat First Division Blackpool 6-3! Memories, memories. All selective ones, of course, and all good ones. What's the point of remembering bad ones? UP THE IRON!

TOMMY TIERNAN

COMEDIAN

I started supporting Liverpool Football Club the day before they lost the 1977 FA Cup final against Manchester Utd, but I was healed four days later when Tommy Smith and co. rose to crush the Gladbachs of Borussia.

It's been an epic journey ever since: Milk Cups, getting the Saturday results, singing in front of the telly, listening to the radio for the European matches in the '80s. I wept on my first visit to Anfield when the Kop sang THAT song. I texted all of my friends at half-time during THAT match to say, "You've got to believe."

I wanted Houillier to go and go dramatically towards the end; no more draws and loose victories, I wanted loss and him gone. Gerrard is a force of nature, Carra is the word made flesh, and I believe in Robbie Fowler's legs and King Kenny's hips. A good win gives me three or four days of peace and glee, but a loss and I can't read the papers the next day. It is an ongoing and everlasting passion, and my kids are Reds now too. I want 'Walk On' written on my tombstone.

RUBY TURNER

SINGER

I don't really support a team as such. I have in the past been taken with the skills of Manchester United in their glory days. Hanging around people who love them can also sway you. Of course my World Cup favourite is the mighty Brazil - that's the game I have to watch when it comes round every four years. A long time to wait but worth it to see the master at work.

RACHEL UNITT

LADIES ENGLAND INTERNATIONAL FOOTBALLER

I follow the results of all my local teams and like them to do well - these are Walsall, West Brom and Wolves - but apart from that I don't really support any one team.

I appreciate good football and like to watch teams for certain players, i.e. Chelsea for John Terry, Man Utd because of Ronaldo and Barcelona to see Ronaldinho.

REG VARNEY

ACTOR

I was born in the East End of London in 1916, so it will come as no surprise to you that my favourite football team is West Ham United, who I have supported since a boy.

My favourite player would have to be Bobby Moore, who I have met and who was a lovely person as well as a great player.

I wish you every success with your book.

RICKY VILLA
FORMER FOOTBALLER

My favourite team is the Argentinean side San lonenzo Sa.

JEREMY VINE
RADIO PRESENTER

My favourite team is Chelsea.

My favourite player is Gianfranco Zola. My biggest regret is not seeing him score the back-flick, jumping, volleyed goal against Norwich in the FA Cup in 2002. I was presenting 'Newsnight' that night.

I have been a season ticket holder at Chelsea since 1996; I joined because I had no clue about football and there was a good tube connection.

TIM VINE

COMEDIAN

My favourite team are Brazil in the World Cup 1982. I loved the way Socrates took penalties - incredible. He stood directly behind the ball with no run-up or even a step in, then he lifted up his leg and scored. I also liked Zico very much even then when I think perhaps he was past his best.

My favourite footballer by an absolute mile is Gazza. He was by far the best dribbler of the ball ever. A lot of rubbish is written about George Best and Maradona - the best ever, and certainly the most underrated footballer of all time, is Gazza.

JEREMY WADE

AUTHOR & TV PRESENTER

When I was a 12-year-old left back playing for my school in rural Suffolk, our very successful team were coached by IPSWICH TOWN player (and former Scotland international) Mick McNeil. Whether this was just good local PR for the club or whether they were that strapped for cash that they had to send players out for second jobs, I don't know. My brother, a few years younger than me, was coached by Brian Talbot and future England captain Mick Mills.

Ipswich is also where I was born. So even after leaving East Anglia, I continued to follow the Town, particularly in the early '70s, when (managed by Bobby Robson) they consistently finished in the League's top four. To be right up there with the big-spending giants was an incredible achievement for a small country club that had no option but to rely mostly on local talent. But it wasn't just about results: they played with great boldness and style, and had some outstanding individual players.

I didn't get to see them play live very often, but the player who particularly sticks in my mind from those occasions is KEVIN BEATTIE. He appeared to defy gravity, soaring to unbelievable heights above the defence and letting nothing past in the air. Moving up for corners and set pieces, he could also be devastating in aerial attack - I saw him thump in two against Sheffield United. His England call-up was inevitable, and he seemed destined for much greater things, but injury deprived him, and us, of the full flowering of this prodigious talent.

Nowadays I'm more likely to be watching two teams of Amazon fishermen playing in a jungle clearing. One game that springs to mind (floating houses and huts on stilts versus huts on dry land) featured two one-legged goalkeepers. One of them, the brother of a friend of mine, who had shot his leg off in a hunting accident, would advance at speed on his crutches then fling them down to dive at the feet of attackers - who had learned to make no allowance for this handicap. I have been persuaded to take part in a few games, but playing against Brazilians is a humiliating experience, even if it's a veterans' game or village free-for-all. They play out of a sheer love of the game, with verve and athleticism, and usually with no thought of being 'discovered' or turning pro - and that's why the national team consistently trounce countries (such as our own) that take it all too seriously.

In fact, now that I think about it, there are echoes in Brazilian football of what I saw in that Ipswich team of the '70s: a heartening reminder, in a hard-nosed world, that success doesn't always have to be the preserve of the economic big hitters.

STEPHANIE WARING

ACTRESS

As I have been a Man U fan ever since I can remember, I used to watch the games with my dad when I was little and I have always made an effort to watch the games as I have got older.

My favourite player used to be Beckham, and not just cos he was cute! He knew what he was doing on the pitch! Now I like Rooney and have always had a soft spot for Ryan Giggs!

NEIL WARNOCK

FOOTBALL MANAGER

My favourite team has always been Sheffield United and my favourite player was Joe Shaw.

Good luck with your fund-raising.

FARA WILLIAMS

LADIES ENGLAND INTERNATIONAL FOOTBALLER

My favourite team are Chelsea, as when I was a kid I was brought up in a Chelsea house and they were also my local team.

My favourite players are Claude Makélélé and Michael Essien, both strong, powerful and strong on the ball whilst making the game look easy.

SHAUN WILLIAMSON

ACTOR

As a 10-year-old, I was very excited when George Best and Rodney Marsh joined Fulham in 1976. The team already boasted the likes of Bobby Moore and Alan Mullery so I plumped for them as 'my team'.

Well, within a year they'd all left! Every man-jack of them, and I was lumbered with a distinctly average team for 'twenty years on hurt'. Great to see them back in the top flight!

BOB WILSON

FORMER FOOTBALLER

My favourite football teams are Chesterfield and Arsenal.

My favourite player was Bert Tramann.

NIGEL WINTERBURN

FORMER FOOTBALLER

My favourite football team is Leeds United.

CHRIS WOODS

FORMER FOOTBALL PLAYER

Favourite team - Chelsea.

I thought Charlie Cooke was brilliant, Alan Hudson, and Iain Hutchinson for his long-throw, windmill arms.

Also Aston Villa because my great uncle Eric Houghton played and was manager there.

ANTONY WORRALL THOMPSON, MOGB

CHEF

Tottenham Hotspur - favourite football team.

I have supported this team since I was a very young boy when I was held high on someone's shoulders to see the game - and I didn't have the privilege of having seats! I remember all the greats: Mackay, Jones, Greaves and Blanchflower.

Whilst I never lived in the area, and I don't often get chance to see them now, they always have been my favourite team. I guess like all the misguided people (!) who support Manchester United, most of them don't actually come from the area.

My favourite all-time player was Dave Mackay, although I had a soft spot (not literally) for fullback, Cyril Knowles because of the memorable football song - 'Nice one son, Nice one Cyril, Let's have another one', which I remember was turned into an advertisement jingle for a sliced white loaf in later years!

NO INTEREST ...

The following celebrities were kind enough to reply but did not have a favourite football team or any interest in football:

* Paul Daniels
* Geoffrey Durham
* Mark Evans
* Michael Fish
* Tony Hart
* James Hawkins
* Ian Hislop
* Bob Holness
* Matthew Kelly
* Kathy Kirby
* John Motson (he felt he could not give a team as a unbiased commentator)
* Sir Stirling Moss MBE
* Jonathan Pryce
* Carol Smilie
* Rick Stein
* Alan Titchmarsh
* Ann Widdecombe
* Archbishop of Canterbury Rowan Williams

OTHER CELEBRITIES ...

I have found out which football teams the following celebrities support/follow, these were obtained by reading various interviews, websites and talking to them in person:

Victoria Adams
Singer
Manchester United

Bertie Aherne
Irish Prime Minister
Manchester United

Donna Air
TV Presenter
Newcastle United

Kriss Akabusi
Former Athlete
West Ham United

Damon Albarn
Singer
Chelsea

John Alderton
Actor
Hull City

Terry Alderton
TV Presenter
Southend United

Fiona Alen
Actress
Bolton Wanderers

Jim Alexander
Actor
Crystal Palace

Benny Anderson
Singer
Arsenal

Clive Anderson
TV Presenter
Arsenal

Howard Antony
Actor
Queens Park Rangers

Natalie Appleton
Singer
Arsenal

John Arlott
Cricket Commentator
Reading

Steven Arnold
Actor
Manchester United

Ray Ashcroft
Actor
Sheffield United

Richard Ashcroft
Solo Artist
Manchester United

Sam Aston
Actor
Burnley

Michael Atherton
Ex Cricket Captain
Manchester United

Sir Richard Attenborough
Actor
Chelsea

Mel B
Singer
Leeds United

Richard Bacon
TV/Radio Presenter
Mansfield Town

David Baddiel
Comedian
Chelsea

Bill Bailey
Comedian
Queens Park Rangers

Colin Baker
Actor
Wycombe Wanderers

Danny Baker
DJ
Millwall

Peter Baker
Golfer
Wolverhampton Wanderers

Ted Baker
Fashion Designer
Tottenham Hotspur

Johnny Ball
TV Presenter
Liverpool

Zoe Ball
TV Presenter
Manchester United

Tony Banks
MP
Chelsea

Carol Barnes
News Presenter
Norwich City

Amanda Barry
Actress
Manchester City

Sean Bean
Actor
Sheffield United

Bill Beaumont
Ex England Rugby Captain
Blackpool

Dani Behr
TV Presenter
Arsenal

Nigel Benn
Boxer
Arsenal

Tony Benn
Politician
Chesterfield

Lenny Bennett
Comedian
Blackpool

Michael Bentt
Boxer
Millwall

Nick Berry
Actor
West Ham United

Martin Bicknell
England Cricketer
Leeds United

Ainsley Bingham
Boxer
Manchester United

Gemma Bissix
Actress
Chelsea

Chris Bisson
Actor
Manchester United

Cilla Black
Presenter
Liverpool

Honor Blackman
Actress
Newcastle United

Tony Blair MP
Former Prime Minister
Newcastle United

Melanie Blatt
Singer
Manchester United

David Blunkett
Politician
Sheffield Wednesday

Bono
U2 Frontman
Celtic

Brandon Block
DJ/Producer
Tottenham Hotspur

Paul Boardman
TV Presenter
Liverpool

Stan Boardman
Comedian
Liverpool

Ian Bolton
Presenter
Chelsea

Nigel Bond
Snooker Player
Manchester City

Ian Botham
Former Cricketer
Scunthorpe United

Frank Bough
TV Presenter
Stoke City

Edith Bowman
Radio/TV Presenter
Manchester United

Max Boyce
Comedian
Swansea City

Peter Brackley
Football Commentator
Brighton & Hove Albion

Melvin Bragg
TV Presenter
Carlisle United

Russel Brand
Comedian & TV Presenter
West Ham United

Jeff Brazier
TV Presenter
Tottenham Hotspur

Lee Brennan
Singer
Carlisle United

Johnny Briggs
Actor
Burnley

Dougie Brimson
Author
Watford

Eric Bristow
Darts Player
Chelsea

Tim Brooke-Taylor
TV Presenter
Derby County

Ray Brooks
Actor
Fulham

Ralph Brown
Actor
Brighton & Hove Albion

Roy 'Chubby' Brown
Comedian
Middlesbrough

Ken Bruce
Radio Presenter
Rangers

Frank Bruno
Retired Boxer
West Ham United

Colin Buchanan
Actor
Birmingham City

Emma Bunton
Singer
Tottenham Hotspur

Gordon Burns
TV Presenter
Manchester United

Milandra Burrows
Actress
Leeds United

Gary Bushell
Newspaper Columnist
Charlton Athletic

Mark Butcher
Cricketer
Crystal Palace

Max Bygraves
Entertainer
Millwall

Richard Caborn
Politician
Sheffield United

Michael Caine
Actor
Chelsea

Andy Cameron
Comedian
Rangers

Rhona Cameron
Comedienne
Celtic

Alistair Campbell
Tony Blair's Press Secretary
Burnley

Darren Campbell
Athlete
Manchester United

Tommy Cannon
Comedian
Rochdale

Julia Carling
TV Presenter
Northampton Town

Robert Carlyle
Actor
Rangers

Harry Carpenter
Boxing Commentator
Crystal Palace

Jasper Carrott
Comedian
Birmingham City

Willie Carson
Retired Jockey
Swindon Town

Alex Carter
Actor
Oldham Athletic

Todd Carty
Actor
West Ham United

Mike Cattermole
TV Presenter
Derby County

Helen Chamberlain
TV Presenter
Torquay United

Ed Chamberlin
Sports Betting Expert
Southampton

Jon Champion
Football Commentator
York City

Jackie Chan
Actor
Arsenal

Mark Chapman
Sports Reporter
Manchester United

Craig Charles
Comedian
Liverpool

Mark Charnock
Actor
Manchester United

Gareth Chilcott
Former England Rugby International
Bristol City

Mel Chisholm
Singer
Liverpool

Chuckle Brothers (The)
Comedians
Rotherham United

Darren Clarke
Golfer
Liverpool

Kenneth Clarke
Politician
Notts County

Jeremy Clarkson
Presenter
Doncaster Rovers

Martin Clunes
Actor
Queens Park Rangers

Sebastian Coe
Athlete/MP
Chelsea

David Coleman
Sports Commentator
Wolverhampton Wanderers

Paul Collingwood
England Cricketer
Sunderland

Phil Collins
Musician
Tottenham Hotspur

Robbie Coltrane
Actor
Celtic

Al Comby
TV Presenter
Celtic

Brian Conley
Comedian
Watford

Billy Connolly
Comedian
Celtic

Ronnie Corbett
Comedian
Crystal Palace

Dominic Cork
Test Cricketer
Stoke City

Phil Cornwell
Comedian/Actor
Tottenham Hotspur

Antony Costa
Singer
Tottenham Hotspur

Tom Courtney
Actor
Hull City

Daniel Craig
Actor
Liverpool

Thomas Craig
Actor
Sheffield Wednesday

Steve Cram
Former Athlete
Sunderland

Michael Crawford
Actor
Crewe Alexandra

Dominic Dale
Snooker Player
Cardiff City

Kelly Dalglish
Newsreader
Liverpool

Lawrence Dallaglio
Former Rugby Player
Chelsea

Roger Daltrey
Actor/Singer
Arsenal

Ian Darke
Sports Commentator
Portsmouth

Craig David
Singer
Southampton

Jim Davidson
Comedian
Charlton Athletic

Alan Davies
Actor
Arsenal

Dickie Davies
TV Sports Presenter
Southampton

Laura Davies
Golfer
Liverpool

Neil Davies
Actor
Liverpool

Matt Dawson
Rugby Player
Everton

Kevin Day
Comedian
Crystal Palace

Simon Day
Comedian
West Ham United

Angus Deayton
TV Presenter/Actor
Manchester United

Chris De Burgh
Singer/Musician
Liverpool

Cat Deeley
TV Presenter
West Bromwich Albion

Keith Deller
Former World Darts Champion
Ipswich Town

Cathy Dennis
Singer
Norwich City

Les Dennis
TV Presenter
Liverpool

Victoria Derbyshire
Radio 5 Live Presenter
Bolton Wanderers

Frankie Dettori
Jockey
Arsenal & Juventus

Dominik Diamond
TV & Radio Presenter
Celtic

Dido
Singer
Arsenal

Jonathan Dimbleby
TV Presenter
Tranmere Rovers

Fred Dinenage
TV Presenter
Portsmouth

Reece Dinsdale
Actor
Huddersfield Town

Pete Doherty
Singer
Queens Park Rangers

Declan Donnelly
TV Presenter
Newcastle United

Danny Dyer
Actor
West Ham United

Robbie Earle
Former Footballer
Port Vale

Peter Ebdon
Snooker Player
Rushden & Diamonds

Stefan Edberg
Retired Tennis Player
Leeds United

Steve Edge
Comedian
Wolverhampton Wanderers

Ade Edmondson
Actor
Queens Park Rangers

Jack Ellis
Actor
Arsenal

Sophie Ellis-Bextor
Singer
Norwich City

Jennifer Ellison
Actress
Everton

Louis Emerick
Actor
Liverpool

David Essex
Musician
West Ham United

Chris Eubank
Retired Boxer
Newcastle United

Lee Evans
Comedian & Actor
Liverpool

Gaynor Faye
Actress
Leeds United

Paul 'Bubble' Ferguson
Presenter
Chelsea

Colin Firth
Actor
Arsenal

Neil Fitzmaurice
Comedy Actor
Liverpool

Stephen Fleming
New Zealand Cricket Captain
Stoke City

Andrew 'Freddie' Flintoff
England Cricket Captain
Manchester City

Carl Fogarty
Former World Superbike Champion
Blackburn Rovers

Michael Foot
Former Leader of the Labour Party
Plymouth Argyle

Emma Forbes
TV Presenter
Bolton Wanderers

Andy 'The Viking' Fordham
Darts Player
Rangers

Alastair Forsythe
Golfer
Rangers

Neil Fouldes
Snooker Player
Queens Park Rangers

Derek Fowlds
Actor
Chelsea

John Francombe
Retired Jockey
Swindon Town

Ben Freeman
Actor
Leeds United

Dawn French
Comedy Actress
Plymouth Argyle

Stephen Fry
Comedian
Norwich City

James Gaddas
Actor
West Ham United

Dean Gaffney
Actor
Brentford

Kirsty Gallagher
Newsreader
Liverpool

Liam Gallagher
Singer/Musician
Manchester City

Noel Gallagher
Singer/Musician
Manchester City

George Galloway
Politician
Celtic

Kate Garraway
TV Presenter
Gillingham

George Gavin
Sports Reporter
Everton

Ruth Gemmell
Actress
Darlington

Ricky Gervais
Comedian/Actor
Reading

Nick Gillingham
Swimmer
Walsall

Nicholas Gleaves
Actor
Bolton Wanderers

Michael Gomez
Boxer
Manchester City

Darren Gough
England Cricketer
Barnsley

David Gower
Former Cricketer
Southampton

Leslie Grantham
Actor
West Ham United

Michael Greco
Actor
Chelsea

Alan Green
Radio Commentator
Macclesfield Town

Robson Green
Actor
Newcastle United

Simon Groom
Presenter
Derby County

Jo Guest
Model
Arsenal

Damon Hague
Boxer
Derby County

David Haig
Actor
Southampton

Stuart Hall
Reporter & Presenter
Manchester City

Geri Halliwell
Singer
Watford

Alan Halsall
Actor
Manchester United

David Hamilton
DJ
Fulham

Natasha Hamilton
Singer
Liverpool

Alex Hammond
News Presenter
Sheffield United

Martin Hancock
Actor
West Ham United

Nick Hancock
Comedian/TV Presenter
Stoke City

Nigel Harman
Actor
Crystal Palace

Dave Harold
Snooker Player
Stoke City

Bob Harris
DJ
Northampton Town

Audley Harrison
Boxer
Arsenal

Roy Hattersley
Politician
Sheffield Wednesday

Ricky Hatton
Boxer
Manchester City

Austin Healey
England Rugby Union International
Everton

Tim Healy
Actor
Newcastle United

Ted Heath
Former Prime Minister
Burnley

Michelle Heaton
Singer
Newcastle United

Malcolm Hebdon
Actor
Burnley

Tim Henman
Tennis Player
Oxford

Lenny Henry
Comedian
West Bromwich Albion

Johnny Herbert
Former F1 Driver
Chelsea

John Higgins
Snooker World Champion
Celtic

Huw Higginson
Actor
Chelsea

Michael Higgs
Actor
Chelsea

Melanie Hill
Actress
Sunderland

Chas Hodges
Singer
Tottenham Hotspur

Kate Hoey
MP
Arsenal

Noddy Holder
Singer
Wolverhampton Wanderers

John Holmes
Actor
Bradford City

Kelly Holmes
Former Athlete
Charlton Athletic

Ken Hom
Chef & Author
Leeds United

Mark Homer
Actor
Arsenal

Geoff Hoon
Politician
Derby County

Jeff Hordley
Actor
Manchester City

Nick Hornby
Author
Arsenal

Andrew Howard
Actor
Cardiff City

Karl Howman
Actor
Charlton Athletic

Mick Hucknall
Singer
Manchester United

Roy Hudd
Comedian
Crystal Palace

Charlotte Hudson
Presenter
Sheffield Wednesday

Sean Hughes
Comedian
Crystal Palace

Lee Hurst
Comedian
West Ham United

Nasser Hussain
England Cricketer
Leeds United

Eric Idle
Actor
Wolverhampton Wanderers

Mark Illot
Cricketer
Watford

Ralph Ineson
Actor
Leeds United

Eddie Irvine
Former Formula 1 Racing Driver
Rangers

Eddie Izzard
Comedian
Crystal Palace

Elton John
Singer
Watford

Joe Johnson
Former Snooker World Champion
Bradford City

Martin Johnson
England Rugby captain
Leicester City

Sue Johnston
Actress
Liverpool

Bruce Jones
Actor
Manchester City

Griff Rhys Jones
Comedian
Ipswich Town

Patricia Jones
Actress
Newcastle United

Ulrika Jonsson
TV Presenter
Manchester United

Phill Jupitus
Comedian
West Ham United

Kerry Katona
Singer
Manchester United

Vernon Kay
TV/Radio Presenter
Bolton Wanderers

Craig Kelly
Actor
Liverpool

Danny Kelly
Radio Presenter
Tottenham Hotspur

Gary Kemp
Actor
Arsenal

Martin Kemp
Actor
Arsenal

Ross Kemp
Actor
West Ham United

Kevin Kennedy
Actor
Manchester City

Patsy Kensit
Actress
Tottenham Hotspur

Jim Kerr
Singer
Celtic

Richard Keys
Presenter
Coventry City

Amir Khan
Olympic Boxing Silver Medallist
Bolton Wanderers

Patrick Kielty
TV Presenter
Manchester United

Terry Kiely
Actor
Manchester United

Neil Kinnock
Former Leader of the Opposition
Cardiff City

Myleene Klass
Singer/Musician & Presenter
Norwich City

Beverley Knight
Singer
Wolverhampton Wanderers

Eric Knowles
TV Presenter
Burnley

Reggie Kray
Former Gangster
Arsenal

Jeremy Kyle
TV Presenter
West Ham United

Steve Lamacq
DJ
Colchester United

Glenn Lamont
Actor
Leeds United

Andrew Lancel
Actor
Everton

Eddie Large
Comedian
Manchester City

Jude Law
Actor
Tottenham Hotspur

Alex Lawler
Actor
Manchester United

George Layton
Actor
Bradford City

Rusty Lee
Chef
Leicester City

Michael Le Vell
Actor
Manchester United

Lennox Lewis
World Champion Boxer
West Ham United

Andy Linden
Actor
Tottenham Hotspur

Sally Lindsay
Actress
Manchester City

Robert Lindsay
Actor
Derby County

Ray Liotta
Actor
Tottenham Hotspur

Ralf Little
Comedy Actor
Manchester United

Richard Littlejohn
Journalist & TV Presenter
Tottenham Hotspur

Hugh Lloyd
Actor
Chester City

Tony Lloyd
Politician
Manchester United

Julian Lloyd Webber
Musician
Leyton Orient

Gabby Logan
Presenter
Leeds United

Kenny Logan
Rugby International
Rangers

Donal Logue
Actor/Comedian
Tottenham Hotspur

Matt Lorenzo
Newsreader
West Ham United

Angus Loughran
Football Statistician
Altrincham

Tim Lovejoy
Presenter
Chelsea

Matt Lucas
Comedian
Arsenal

Zoe Lucker
Actress
Huddersfield Town

Lulu
Singer
Rangers

Des Lynam
Presenter
Brighton & Hove Albion

Kenny Lynch
Comedian
Brentford

Paul McCartney
Musician
Everton

Robert McCracken
Boxer
Birmingham City

John McCririck
TV Racing Presenter
Newcastle United

Ian McCulloch
Snooker Player
Preston North End

Brian McFadden
Singer
Coventry City

Steve McFadden
Actor
Manchester United

Alistair McGowan
Comedian
Coventry City

Rory McGrath
Comedian
Arsenal

Barry McGuigan
Former Boxer
Tottenham Hotspur

Patrick McGuinness
Comedian
Bolton Wanderers

Mike MacLean
TV Presenter
Manchester City

Alan McManus
Snooker Player
Celtic

Anthony McPartlin
TV Presenter
Newcastle United

Ian McShane
Actor
Manchester United

John Major
Former Prime Minister
Chelsea

Timmy Mallett
TV Presenter
Oxford

Bernard Manning
Comedian
Manchester City

Nigel Mansell
Former Formula One Champion
Exeter City

Clive Mantle
Actor
Chelsea

Vicky Marsden
Radio One DJ
Blackburn Rovers

Connor Marsh
Actor
Bolton Wanderers

Michelle Marsh
Model
Oldham Athletic

Simon Mayo
DJ
Tottenham Hotspur

Lucy Meacock
TV Presenter
Chester City

David Mellor
Former MP
Chelsea

Jayne Middlemiss
TV Presenter
AFC Bournemouth

Philip Middlemiss
Actor
Hartlepool United

John Middleton
Actor
Wolverhampton Wanderers

Colin Miller
Australian Cricketer
Blackburn Rovers

Bob Mills
Presenter
Leyton Orient

Scott Mills
Radio One Presenter
Southampton

Heather Mills-McCartney
Former Model
Sunderland

Warren Mitchell
Actor
Tottenham Hotspur

Colin Montgomerie
Golfer
Leeds United & Rangers

Brian Moore
Commentator
Gillingham

Mark Moraghan
Actor
Liverpool

Nick Moran
Actor
Arsenal

Desmond Morris
Author
Oxford

Mark Morrison
Singer
Leicester City

Neil Morrissey
Comedy Actor
Crystal Palace

Guy Mowbray
Football Commentator
York City

Alison Moyet
Singer/Musician
Southend United

Chris Moyles
Radio/TV Presenter
Leeds United

Dermot Murnaghan
Newsreader
Everton

Glen Murphy
Actor
West Ham United

Colin Murray
TV/Radio Presenter
Liverpool

Patrick Murray
Actor
Millwall

Mike Myers
Comedian
Liverpool

Jimmy Nail
Actor
Newcastle United

Shea Neary
Boxer
Everton

David Neilson
Actor
Leicester City

Johnny Nelson
Boxer
Sheffield Wednesday

Trevor Nelson
TV/Radio Presenter
Chelsea

Gary Newbon
Reporter & Interviewer
Leicester City

Charlie Nicholas
Former Football Player
Celtic

Paul Nicholls
Actor
Bolton Wanderers

Bill Nighy
Actor
Crystal Palace

Emma Noble
Model
Arsenal

Barry Norman
TV Presenter
Tottenham Hotspur

Steven Norris
Politician
Fulham

Stephen North
Actor
Brighton & Hove Albion

Kerry Norton
Actress
Arsenal

Paul Oakenfold
DJ
Chelsea

Tony Oakey
Boxer
Portsmouth

Des O'Connor
TV Presenter
Northampton Town

Tom O'Connor
Comedian
Everton

Martin Offiah
Rugby Player
Manchester United

Ardal O'Hanlon
Comedian
Leeds United

Dermot O'Leary
TV Presenter
Arsenal

Jamie Oliver
Chef
Cambridge United

Jo O'Meara
Singer
West Ham United

Paul Opacic
Actor
Halifax Town

Tony O'Shea
Darts Player
Stockport County

Ronnie O'Sullivan
Snooker Player
Arsenal

Greg Owen
Golfer
Nottingham Forest

Mark Owen
Singer
Liverpool

Nick Owen
TV Presenter
Luton Town

Chris Packham
TV Presenter
Southampton

Kevin 'The Artist' Painter
Darts Player
Ipswich Town

Arnold Palmer
Golf Legend
Rangers

John Parrott
Snooker Player
Everton

Andrew Paul
Actor
Arsenal

Heather Peace
Actress
Bradford City

Dave Peacock
Singer
Tottenham Hotspur

Jonathan Pearce
Football Commentator
Bristol City

Adam Pearson
Author
Southampton

Neil Pearson
Actor
Tottenham Hotspur

Steve Pemberton
Actor
Blackburn Rovers

Sue Perkins
TV Presenter
Newcastle United

Fiona Phillips
TV Presenter
Southampton

Leslie Phillips
Actor
Tottenham Hotspur

Steven Pinder
Actor
Blackburn Rovers

Gary Player
Golfer
Rangers

Sue Pollard
Actress
Nottingham Forest

Pete Postlethwaite
Actor
Shrewsbury Town

Ian Poulter
Golfer
Arsenal

HRH Prince Andrew
Norwich City

HRH Prince Harry
Arsenal

HRH Prince William
Aston Villa

Gordon Ramsey
Chef
Rangers

Daniel Ratcliffe
Actor
Fulham

Ian Reddington
Actor
Sheffield Wednesday

Vic Reeves
Comedian
Darlington

Jonny Regan
Big Brother Contestant
Sunderland

John Reid
Politician
Celtic

Mike Reid
Comedian
Millwall

Mike Reid
DJ
Bury

Dean Reynolds
Snooker Player
Grimsby Town

Gary Rhodes
Chef
Manchester United

Eric Richard
Actor
Arsenal

Adam Rickett
Actor
Manchester City

Lisa Riley
Actress
Manchester United

Shane Ritchie
TV Presenter
Manchester United

Natalie Robb
Actress
Celtic

Sam Robertson
Actor
Liverpool

Ted Robbins
Comedian
Wrexham

Tony Robinson
Actor/TV Presenter
Bristol City

Lisa Rogers
Actress
Arsenal

Jim Rosenthal
Sports Commentator
Oxford

Paul Ross
TV Presenter
West Ham United

Patricia Routledge
Actress
Tranmere Rovers

Jack Russell
Former Cricketer
Forest Green Rovers

Jack Ryder
Actor
Newcastle United

Kym Ryder
Singer
Manchester United

Steve Ryder
Presenter
Charlton Athletic

Fabrice Santoro
French Tennis Player
Chelsea

Sunetra Sarker
Actress
Liverpool

Jennifer Saunders
Comedienne
Manchester United

Phillip Schofield
TV Presenter
Cardiff City

Jenny Seagrove
Actress
Everton

Martin Shaw
Actor
Aston Villa

Tracy Shaw
Actress
Derby County

Ben Shephard
TV Presenter
West Ham United

Charlie Simpson
Singer
Ipswich Town

Jane Sixsmith
Hockey Player
Aston Villa

Frank Skinner
Comedian
West Bromwich Albion

Chris Smith
MP
Arsenal

Christopher Smith
Actor
Bradford City

Delia Smith
TV Chef
Norwich City

Mel Smith
Comedian
Arsenal

David Sneddon
Singer
Rangers

John Snow
TV Presenter
Brighton & Hove Albion

Hannah Spearitt
Singer
Norwich City

Dave Spikey
Comedian
Bolton Wanderers

Kathy Staff
Actress
Huddersfield Town

John Stapleton
TV Presenter
Manchester City

David Starie
Boxer
Ipswich Town

Freddie Starr
Comedian
Everton

Jeff Stelling
TV/Radio Presenter
Hartlepool United

Nicola Stephenson
Actress
Oldham Athletic

Rachel Stevens
Singer
Arsenal

Alec Stewart
England Test Cricketer
Chelsea

Patrick Stewart
Actor
Huddersfield Town

Rod Stewart
Singer
Celtic

Joss Stone
Singer
Liverpool

Graeme Storm
Golfer
Hartlepool United

Jack Straw
MP
Blackburn Rovers

Ray Stubbs
Sports Presenter
Tranmere Rovers

Joe Swash
Actor
Arsenal

Claire Sweeney
Actress
Everton

Jimmy Tarbuck
Comedian
Liverpool

John Taylor
Guitarist
Aston Villa

Phil Taylor
Darts Player
Port Vale

Teddy Taylor
Politician
Southend United

Jamie Theakston
TV/Radio Presenter
Brighton & Hove Albion

Sarah Thomas
Supermodel
Norwich City

Simon Thomas
Presenter
Norwich City

Willie Thorne
Snooker Player
Leicester City

Daley Thompson
Olympic Gold Medal Decathlete
Mansfield Town

Pete Tong
DJ
Arsenal

Stephen Tompkinson
Actor
Middlesbrough

Sam Torrance
Golfer
Celtic

Brian Travers
Saxophonist
Aston Villa

Bill Treacher
Actor
Ipswich Town

Marcus Trescothick
England Cricketer
Bristol City

Phil Tuffnell
Former Cricketer
Arsenal

Cheryl Tweedy
Singer
Newcastle United

Clive Tyldsley
Football Commentator
Everton

Martin Tyler
Football Commentator
Woking

Michael Underwood
TV Presenter
Northampton Town

Johnny Vaughan
Comedian
Chelsea

Johnny Vegas
Comedian
Liverpool

Tim Vincent
Actor
Wrexham

John Virgo
Snooker Player
Manchester United

Bradley Walsh
Actor
Arsenal

Rick Wakeman
Musician
Manchester City

Anna Walker
TV Presenter
Sheffield United

Alex Walkinshaw
Actor
West Ham United

Rik Waller
Pop Idol Contestant
Gillingham

Tommy Walsh
Ground Force Gardener
West Ham United

Bill Ward
Actor
Newcastle United

Frank Warren
Boxing Promoter
Arsenal

Dennis Waterman
Actor
Chelsea

Pete Waterman
Musician
Walsall

Mike Watkinson
Former England Cricketer
Bolton Wanderers

Denise Welsh
Actress
Newcastle United

Lee Westwood
Golfer
Nottingham Forest

John White
Author
Manchester United

Paul Whitehouse
Comedian
Tottenham Hotspur

Roger Whittaker
Singer
Hereford United

Andrew Whyment
Actor
Manchester United

Jonathan Wilkes
TV Presenter
Port Vale

Darren Williams
Boxer
Hereford United

Mark Williams
Actor
Aston Villa

Robbie Williams
Singer
Port Vale

Russ Williams
TV/Radio Presenter
Tottenham Hotspur

Sean Wilson
Actor
Manchester United

Barbara Windsor
Actress
Arsenal

Kate Winslett
Actress
Reading

Ray Winstone
Actor
West Ham United

Dale Winton
TV Presenter
Arsenal

Bill Woebernick
Snooker Player
Ipswich Town

Elijah Wood
Actor
West Ham United

Sir Clive Woodward
England World Cup Rugby Union Coach
Chelsea

Adam Woodyatt
Actor
Liverpool

Bill Wyman
Musician
Crystal Palace

Mike Yarwood
Comedian
Stockport County

Kelli Young
Singer
Derby County

Kirsty Young
TV News Presenter
Rangers

Paul Young
Singer
Luton Town

OTHER BOOKS BY CHRIS COWLIN:

The Southend United Quiz Book
Foreword by: Frank Dudley
ISBN: 1-904444-91-1 978-1904444-91-6
Price: £5.99

Will you be a Shrimper with a record catch as you reel in the answers to the 800 tricky questions in this quiz book about Southend United Football Club, or will you be singing the Blues as you bemoan the one, or more, that got away?

Your knowledge about all aspects of the club since its formation will be tested to the limit, from memorable managers and players to transfer fees, opponents, scores, awards and all the unforgettable competitions and matches that have kept fans on the edge of their seats throughout the club's long history.

With a fitting foreword by Frank Dudley, this quiz book is brimming with interesting facts and figures and is guaranteed to provide hours of entertainment, reminiscing and discussion for fans of the club.

The Official Watford Football Club Quiz Book
Foreword by: Graham Taylor OBE
ISBN: 1-904444-85-7 978-1-904444-85-5
Price: £7.99

Be prepared to stir up a veritable hornets nest as you strive to meet the challenge of answering 1,000 testing questions about Watford Football Club. This quiz book certainly has the 'ouch' factor, guaranteeing that even the most ardent fan will get stung several times along the way.

Covering every subject imaginable about the Hornets, from players of old to the most recent Cup competitions, it not only contains a wealth of interesting facts and figures but also will stir up fond memories of all the great personalities and nail-biting matches that have helped to mould the Club throughout its long history.

With a fitting Foreword by legendary Watford Manager, Graham Taylor OBE, this book will provide hours of entertainment for the whole family who, whilst licking their wounds, can console themselves in the knowledge that £1 from the sale of each copy will be donated to the charity Sense, which helps deaf and blind people of all ages lead fuller and happier lives.

The West Ham United Quiz Book
Foreword by: Julian Dicks
ISBN: 1-904444-99-7   978-1-904444-99-2
Price: £6.99

Now is the time to find out how much you West Ham United fans really know, but be warned – your brains are sure to take a hammering as you struggle to answer the 1,000 challenging questions in this quiz book, covering every aspect of the team's history, such as players, managers, opponents, scores, transfers, nationalities and every competition you can think of.

You'll be arguing with the referee and pleading for extra time as the questions spark recollections and ardent discussions of the legendary greats and nail-biting matches that have shaped the club over the years.

With a fitting foreword by Hammers legend Julian Dicks, and bulging with important facts and figures, this book will entertain as well as educate, but be prepared for a few fouls and yellow cards along the way.

The Gooners Quiz Book
Foreword by: Bob Wilson
ISBN: 1-904444-77-6   978-1-904444-77-0
Price: £8.99

Will you do the Gooners proud as you display an impressive knowledge of your favourite club, Arsenal, or will you instead prove yourself to be a complete goon, as trip over your own feet in search of the answers to the 1,000 cunning questions in this quiz book?

Covering every aspect of the club's history from players to managers and from national to international competitions since its foundation over a century ago, and with a fitting Foreword by former Scotland and Arsenal goalkeeping legend and TV presenter, Bob Wilson, this book will challenge Gooners fans of all ages as well as providing fascinating facts and figures both to enthral and to trigger fond memories and ardent discussions.

If you find yourself floundering, you can recover your dignity and find consolation in the fact that £1 from the sale of every book will go to the Willow Foundation, a charity founded by Bob and Megs Wilson and dedicated to arranging individually tailored 'Special Days' for seriously ill young adults.

The Official Norwich City Football Club Quiz Book

Foreword by: Bryan Gunn

ISBN: 1-904444-80-6 978-1-904444-80-0

Price: £8.99

Will you be singing like a Canary as you fly with ease through this book's 1,000 challenging quiz questions about Norwich City Football Club, or will you have flown the Nest too soon and come crashing to the ground spitting feathers?

Covering all aspects of the club's history, including top goalscorers, transfers, managers, Cup competitions, League positions, awards, legendary players and nationalities, it will push to the limit even the most ardent aficionados' knowledge of their favourite team.

With a fitting foreword by the legendary Bryan Gunn, this book is guaranteed to trigger fond recollections of all the nail-biting matches and colourful characters that have shaped the club over the years, as well as providing a wealth of interesting facts and figures with which to impress your friends and family.

The Official Colchester United Quiz Book

Foreword by: Karl Duguid

ISBN: 1-904444-88-1 978-1-904444-88-6

Price: £5.99

Question: How many U's are there in Colchester? Answer: One, of course - as all Colchester United fans ought to know. And, if that little teaser caught you out, then brace yourselves for 700 more tricky questions, relating to your favourite team, the U's.

Covering all aspects of the club, from players and managers to nationalities and every conceivable tournament, you will be required to U's your brainpower to its limit to come up with all the answers and amaze (or otherwise) your friends and family with the depth of your knowledge about the club.

With a fitting Foreword by Karl Duguid, this book will trigger recollections of vourite players past and present, nail-biting matches, and all the club's highs and lows heir long history. A veritable treasure trove of facts and figures is at your enjoy!